Originally from Northern Ireland and now living in London, Annie Caulfield writes plays for theatre, screen and radio. A recent BBC radio play won a Race in the Media Award from the Commission for Racial Equality, and her stage play *Walk the Line* was awarded a Special Prize in the 1994 Manchester Royal Exchange Playwriting Competition. Having written for many TV comedy shows, Annie continues to work regularly as a scriptwriter for comedian Lenny Henry. She has written and broadcast for BBC Radio travel programmes on a variety of destinations, including the Middle East, East Africa and Spain; her travel writing also appears in the *Independent* newspaper. *Kingdom of the Film Stars* is Annie's first book.

KINGDOM
OF THE
FILM STARS

Journey into Jordan

Annie Caulfield

LONELY PLANET PUBLICATIONS
Melbourne • Oakland • London • Paris

Kingdom of the Film Stars: Journey into Jordan

Published by Lonely Planet Publications
    Head Office: PO Box 617, Hawthorn, Vic 3122, Australia
    Branches: 155 Filbert St, Suite 251, Oakland, CA 94607, USA
                 10 Barley Mow Passage, Chiswick, London W4 4PH, UK
                 71 bis rue du Cardinal Lemoine, 75005 Paris, France

Published 1997

Printed by SNP Printing Pte Ltd, Singapore

Author photograph by Woodrow Phoenix

Map by Adam McCrow

National Library of Australia Cataloguing in Publication Data

Caulfield, Annie
Kingdom of the Film Stars: Journey into Jordan

ISBN 0 86442 461 2.

1. Caulfield, Annie – Journeys – Jordan.
2. Jordan – Description and travel. I. Title.
(Series: Lonely Planet Journeys.)

915.69504

Text © Annie Caulfield 1997
Map © Lonely Planet 1997

Inevitably, this book is dedicated to my friend Rathwan.

Acknowledgments

With big thanks to the following folks at home – in alphabetical but equal order of helpfulness and loveliness: Juliet Burton, Simon Calder, James Caulfield, Lenny Henry, Kaisley Phillips, Woodrow Phoenix, Noah Richler, John Rovira, Micheline Steinberg and Mary Walsh. I'd also like to thank all those who helped me and made me feel at home in Jordan; I hope those who recognise themselves as friends in this book will be pleased by the depiction of themselves. For those many who aren't mentioned (just because there weren't nearly enough pages) and for those who wouldn't have the English to read the book, I'd like to send my gratitude anyway, because I met so much kindness that didn't expect thanks. Finally, thanks to all the Lonely Planet crew, Michelle de Kretser in particular.

CONTENTS

In some distant age, there will be no nomads left in Arabia –
but it is still far off I'm glad to think.

Gertrude Bell, 1905

Introduction

There are two things we imagine will happen. Immediate thoughts about Western women and Arab men tend to leap at a couple of clichés and get stuck clinging to them.

In the first, she's swept off her feet by a handsome, heavily armed sheikh on horseback and carried off to a life of exotic, erotic adventure. She'd be wearing wafting silk and he'd probably have a sword between his teeth a lot of the time. The backdrop is an eternally blazing sunset and rolling dunes; the close-ups are hotter than the sand. This is a fantasy that belongs to the past and to advertising.

The second thought, the one for our time and our reality, is conjured from the memory of gruelling documentaries and heart-rending newspaper reports, and there's not much it could be used to advertise. Children abducted by Arab fathers and never returned. The Arab husband, who once seemed so charming, turning into an abusive stranger who expects his Western wife to abandon her culture and live veiled among the wives and children he had back home all along. This sinister picture of the Arab male has been darkened further by our knowledge of the suffering in many Arab women's lives.

This book tells of an exception to all those bleak contemporary tales. I know it's not the only story of its kind to set against the piled images of sadness and pain, but it's a story I haven't heard much lately.

CHAPTER 1

Opening Shots

The hotel I wanted had no address. It had a gilt-embossed business card with a picture of a hotel, and a lot of Arabic script I had always thought was the address but now began to suspect must just say 'We're warm and hospitable, but first you've got to find us'.

My taxi driver reacted to this card in a way I'd seen drivers react before: he looked at it, nodded, set off with confidence and ended up meandering all over the city centre, getting stuck in traffic and asking me to repeat the hotel's name several times, as if the incantation would conjure it up.

It was the day before Christmas Eve and I didn't have enough clothes on. I'd forgotten that it snowed in Amman winters. Heavy, freezing snow, re-roofing mosques and landing on slip-ping, hurrying Bedouin. The geriatric taxi had holes in its floor and no heating. I was already sorry enough for myself and could do without careering eternally around Downtown Amman, losing toes to frostbite, developing hypothermia, listening forever to the driver's tape of a love-tortured Egyptian singer auto-reverse over and over, playing the same songs . . . Of course I wouldn't be careering eternally if I did get hypothermia – I'd die and everyone in Jordan would be very sorry they'd printed trick business cards.

And what had possessed me to come back to Jordan again, when I was still unable to summon enough Arabic to say, "Stop the taxi and call an ambulance, my feet just fell off" or "How come you've got such a flash tape deck and no floor in your car"?

Actually, I had a feeling I knew what had possessed me, crept into me when I'd thought I was just having an adventure.

I'd read about Gertrude Bell, who travelled the deserts of Arabia in the early years of this century to fill the empty wastes that lay between her brief encounters with the very married, very English man she loved. Poor Gertrude, out there alone, charting the deserts, befriending warlike sheikhs and setting up the stage for Lawrence of Arabia. All he had to do was ride through in fluttering, glamorous white; Gertrude had done the real work.

Gertrude wasn't one for the fluttering white. She always dressed in the latest gown from Paris and always wore a fetching hat – at least to the extent that there was anything to be fetched from her too-strong, too long-chinned face. Fearless, a charmer of scarred Arabs with guns on their backs and knives at their belts, she persuaded the sheikhs to let her help make them into puppet kings in the presumptuous carve-up of their lands by the French and English after World War One. They respected her and trusted her – for a while. Then the puppets cut their strings and dropped Gertrude from their social lists. As for English society, it had long tried to pretend it was out when she called. Poor, long-chinned Gertrude – killed herself in Baghdad, no longer useful and never loved.

I went to the desert, charted no charts, kinged no kings and wasn't very brave; but in the humming emptiness of the sands I found something Gertrude was constantly hoping for.

It takes time to see the desert; you have to keep looking at it. When you've looked long enough, you realise the blank wastes of sand and rock are teeming with life. Just as you can keep looking at a person and suddenly realise that the way you see them has completely changed: from being a stranger, they've gradually revealed themselves as someone with a wealth of complexities and surprising subtleties that you're growing to love. I was luckier than Gertrude: when I realised what I felt for my very un-English man, he was feeling exactly the same way about me.

He could do a thing with his eyes: hold me with them until I changed my mind. He wasn't young. He was a boy. He was completely alien. He was familiar. He was optimistic and he was deeply melancholy. He was thoughtless, but in the next moment he'd pre-empt my needs as though I were a small child who might not know how to ask for what I wanted. I saw him as himself; I saw an enigmatic Arabian. Some days, we were brother and sister; some days, passion came stinging through the hot air in a passing glance. I knew it was one of the biggest things in my life; I thought the sun had got to me and I'd romanticised the whole business to make my holiday memories interesting. He never let up in his careful battle to prove he was right for me, but my growing knowledge of him had done more than all his campaigns to bind us together. I kept going back to Jordan. Unlike Gertrude, I was running to, not from.

It had all gone romantically, fascinatingly well. Up till now. Three years after the first look.

Lost in the snow, with my taxi driver losing the will to live as he got caught in yet another of Amman's one-way systems, it occurred to me that although I might have been luckier in love, I wasn't one inch the traveller Gertrude had been. She charged about on a donkey most of the time – that must have been a gale force more draughty in winter than my taxi. She certainly wouldn't have been panicking about not finding her cosy hotel: it was the proper carry-on in tents and caves for Gertrude, even if she did make her Arab porters drag table linen and a full dinner service around the desert so that her Sloane Square standards were kept up wherever she was.

I recognised the street – we were saved. In fact, it was the street that was to blame for everything because it had no name. There was just a general term for this area of Amman and taxi drivers could never really believe that I wanted to go there anyway. Westerners who could afford taxis stayed up in the hills in big hotels; only locals and bus-riding backpackers lurked in the heaving lower depths of the city. The hills had trees, new houses, plate glass, air-conditioning and a clean tranquillity the better-off could retreat to and survey their city as it unravelled towards Downtown, the scruffy valley where a very different life was lived.

Downtown. Where you could eat for pennies and buy cigarettes for a quarter of the European price from Iraqi refugees squatting on the pavement, their wares set out on cardboard boxes or their own threadbare coats. Safeway, McDonalds and Pizza Hut were up in the hills, full of rich, foreign-educated young Arabs who wore Versace, smoked Marlboro and liked to pepper their conversation with American-accented English; Downtown, small dusty Palestinian boys ran about with wooden trays on their heads, piled high with bread and cakes, and old men sold Bedouin coffee from elaborate silver pots as they huddled in doorways with their makeshift wheeled stoves. Cafes curled with the smoke from *narjileh* pipes, fat cracked from pans of felafel cooked at the roadside. Second-hand Western clothes were haggled over by men wearing a hundred variations on traditional Arab dress, while veiled women struggled to cross terrifyingly busy roads with armfuls of babies. Downtown never ceased to be a racket of shouts, traffic, music . . . and didn't pretend to be anything other than itself.

The taxi driver let me off at the Hotel Wadi with an 'on your own head be it' glance at the den I was going into. My head was fine: I'd at least found something in Amman that was exactly where it should be to greet me.

The hotel was reached through a passageway between two brightly lit shoe shops that seemed to provide a twenty-four-hour supply of cheap, sequined, buckled and bedecked ladies' shoes. I'd once gone in trying to buy a pair of plain-as-possible sandals and had horrified the salesmen with my size sevens; whoever they were hoping to sell shoes to at unlikely hours, it certainly wasn't the inelegant likes of me.

At the end of the passageway was a laundry. The steam-wreathed laundry men were surprised to see me. They waved their irons, then returned to pressing comforting warmth into old shirts and dresses for second-hand sale in the street market. Like the shoe-shop men, they didn't seem to sleep, providing used cleanliness long into the night, occasionally shouting encouraging remarks to each other in the battle against the mounds of crumpled material at their feet. Constantly hoping for distraction, they kept a sidelong watch on the hotel stairs to their left; the comings and goings of the hotel guests were always likely to be more interesting than ironing clothes.

Having provided a distraction, I bungled up the narrow stairs with my bags. I noticed that the stair carpet had worn well; it was evidently practical to use lurid Astro-turf instead of conventional carpeting. Two flights of Astro-turf later, there was the reinforced glass door that always stuck. I banged through and, my balance thrown out by my bags, came as near to falling on the reception desk as not-quite-falling could come. Omar was at the desk, startled; he looked behind me, waiting, because obviously Rathwan must be just behind me. When I closed the door, he went into startlement overdrive.

"Rathwan?" he asked, still looking hopefully towards the stairs. Omar didn't like it. Nor did I. Of course I never arrived alone, I knew that.

I'd waited ages at the airport. Once or twice in the past,

Rathwan hadn't been there to greet me, having wandered off to talk to some of his many friends. I'd panicked – "He's not here, he's not here, it's all over . . ." But he'd always be there in the end.

I'd given him over an hour this time, checking the buffet, not meeting the eyes of increasingly curious policemen, reading darker and darker significance into the fact that Rathwan hadn't telephoned me the previous night. He usually called the night before I left, just to check everything was going according to plan; it was part of the ritual. In England, I hadn't set much store by his omission; if he was out in the desert, telephones weren't always handy. But at the airport, his failure to call became a clear omen of disaster. Unfortunately for me, I do have the sort of imagination that assumes that when people are late they've been run over. Or in Rathwan's case, had his throat cut in some Bedouin tribal feud.

I forced myself to think like a reasonable person; probably just some delay getting back from his last tour-guiding job – a small hiccup in our usual schedule and not some appalling tragedy. Before the police moved me on for loitering with a sulky face, I decided to make my way to the hotel. If Rathwan didn't turn up there, I'd go in search of friends of his the following morning – one of them would be bound to know his whereabouts.

Omar asked again, "Rathwan?"

Now we were stuck. I tried to muster the Arabic to explain, but only managed a shrug and a wave of my hands to indicate that something had vanished. Omar understood – perhaps more from my distraught look than from my sign language.

He looked distraught himself: "*Maa fii* rooms." There were no rooms.

"*Maa fii* rooms, Man," Omar repeated with a regretful sigh. This wasn't him trying out his hippest English; 'man' was how he pronounced my name.

I was tired and cold. I suspected I was going to burst into tears. (Sorry, Gertrude.)

"Rathwan?" Omar tried one last baffled enquiry.

"*Wain?*" I asked with a despairing shrug. I really was a dunce at Arabic if the most I could manage after all these years was a pathetic bleat of "Where?" However, the bleat stung Omar's heart. He waved towards the lounge: "Waiting, Man, waiting."

I smiled, took back the threat of tears. Perhaps something could be sorted out.

"Amjad!" Omar yelled in the direction of the little kitchen at the back. "*Chai!*"

Amjad, a small, plump Egyptian, one of two Egyptians who did all the real work in the hotel, beamed when he saw me, then started with the enquiries about Rathwan. Omar explained something, Amjad looked at me with concern and scuttled back to the kitchen.

"Waiting, Man, please." Omar waved me to the lounge again.

The square brown plastic armchairs lining the walls were empty. So where were all these people who'd hogged all the rooms? I'd never seen the lounge empty. Usually it thronged with Iraqis, Kuwaitis, Sudanese, Palestinians, Saudis . . . People from every corner of the Arab world turned up in these brown chairs and could be found at any hour of the day drinking tea, having intense discussions, staring into space or watching television.

The television was the only thing that was as normal, blaring away in the corner, bringing news of some disaster somewhere. Feeling a shade disastrous myself, I took a chair by the window. It was getting dark; the street life outside stepped up its pace as snow-damp workers headed home.

Amjad brought me tea and a sympathetic shake of his head. "Rathwan? *Wain?*"

I made my disappeared-thing gesture and smiled cheerfully, as if the possible death, desertion or disabling of Rathwan meant nothing to me. Amjad scrubbed floors, fetched, carried, slopped out bathrooms and lived on a pittance slightly better than the starvation he'd have faced at home – he didn't need to be worrying his young self with my minor troubles. He did worry though, and moved an ashtray onto the low table in front of me; obviously, I'd be needing a cigarette. I lit one and smiled at Amjad again, trying to convey that really, I was fine. He wandered off to yet more of his ceaseless menial tasks, exuding joy and generosity as always; a full timetable of dirty jobs seemed to have the same effect on Amjad as Ecstasy on the rest of us.

Unchastened by Amjad's example, I sank back into deep gloom about my own situation – gloom darkened by the sentiment attached to the time of year. Here I was, alone, miles from family and friends, presents and turkeys. Here I was in the Middle East just before Christmas, stranded with *maa fii* rooms at the inn. On the street outside some Bedouin were pulling a tarpaulin over a truckload of wet, cold, complaining sheep. There were the shepherds then. But where was my wise man?

There were plenty of other hotels. I could have toured around in a taxi until one of them gave me a stable, but I didn't want to leave the comfortable, cockroachy safe haven of the Hotel Wadi; I felt I just had to trust Omar's faith in waiting. He'd gone from reception, leaving Amjad's sidekick in charge: a huge-muscled Egyptian who everyone called Sylvester Stallone, never tiring of the joke. I waved at Sylvester, he waved back and started talking to Amjad – hearing Rathwan's name, I knew that he too was enquiring about my mysterious solitary arrival.

I waited, and remembered the first time I sat in this lounge wondering about Rathwan's whereabouts, not knowing anyone to wave to, more scared than gloomy. Scared of myself as much as scared that he wouldn't show up; I knew I'd done something pretty stupid.

"You can't go halfway across the world to see a man you hardly know with just loose change in your pocket," my best friend had told me. But I'd done exactly that.

After several years of lucrative television writing, my pockets were surprised to find themselves emptying out. It was my own fault: I wasn't pursuing lucky breaks the way an ambitious television writer should, I wasn't dogging the footsteps of inter-ested producers, wasn't being eager and obliging, fighting a big fight over the positioning of my name in the sacred title credits of comedy shows. I was tired of hacking out gags and sketches; I realised I'd almost stopped putting pen to paper for anything other than a cash deadline. I wanted to get back to the place I'd started from, writing the plays and stories that came out of my own head. All this foot-stamping for artistic integrity and wayward slinging back of good fortune had left me broke and confused. I was probably just going crazy.

Meanwhile, I kept replying to the letters that came from Jordan and answering the telephone calls that came once a fortnight for six months. Heady stuff, considering I'd only known Rathwan for three days. A brief encounter had turned into a major project for him. Why not for me? What else had I got to do but pace the house holding an unpaid tax demand in one hand and an unfinished novel in the other?

I'd met him while I was spending the last of my money on a journey through Egypt and Jordan with a group of travel-hardened Australians. They were being very kind about not killing me as I turned out to be completely useless at all practical aspects of our mucking-in-together camping holiday. We'd left the grubby, verge-of-a-nervous-breakdown crowding that makes Cairo's streets such a wonderful nightmare and had been shocked by the clean beauty of Jordan, with its well-fed, well-spaced people. There was so much cheerfulness, so much air to breathe . . . We raced through the country's main sights, ending up in Amman. The layers of history in the city could occupy the mind for weeks, but we had just three days. Rathwan showed us the surface of the layers, explaining, entertaining and helping us understand a little of the ancient city. I noticed, in passing, that he was very good-looking, powerfully built and dressed in jeans and a checked shirt, more like a cowboy than a Bedouin – but we were there to see old things, not young ones, and time was short.

"The Romans called Amman 'Philadelphia'. The name comes from the Greek, meaning 'brotherly love'. If you follow me now we'll go to the Roman temple of Hercules . . ."

He was used to tourists wanting to grasp thousands of years of culture in moments and led us around at the breakneck pace we wanted, always just ahead of us with his distinctive walk, a sort of determined saunter. I wasn't aware of him paying any special attention to me until the tour was almost over, when he discreetly cut me away from the herd and persuaded me to have dinner with him, holding my attention with those eyes of his, eyes a young Omar Sharif would have envied.

My particular friend on the tour was a burly female officer in the Australian army. She stood by the taxi door when Rathwan collected me, warning him that she'd be waiting up for me. He laughed and said, "You can come too if you're worried."

He got a stern glare. He responded to it with a gushing promise that he respected all women, that he was a Bedouin, that it was his culture to respect all women . . . My friend muttered – and I thought – "Bullshit."

At dinner, he fussed over every mouthful I ate in case it might not be quite right. He told me about places in Jordan I wouldn't have time to see on this trip, he told me about his life, a little. He made me laugh a great deal as we talked in the lantern-lit, open-air restaurant with vines curling round lattices and a fountain playing by our table. Romantic? If he wanted to be sure I'd go soft in the head he couldn't have designed a better restaurant himself.

I was able to report back to my Australian bodyguard that this particular smooth-talking Bedouin didn't start a wrestling match on the first date: he simply shook hands and looked at me for a very long time. No sudden moves on the second date either. The same easy chat, the same staring into my soul. He knew I was leaving the next day and I found myself promising to write, to come back.

Two dates. Two dates filled with hours of bonding you'd never get in years with some people – half my head said this as I left Amman. The other half told me it was very hot, that this sort of thing happened on holiday and that my romantic ravings would be cured by a strong blast of the cold, sensible English air waiting outside Heathrow Airport.

No famed or fabled desert warrior ever mounted a siege like Rathwan's campaign to get me back to Jordan. I repeatedly pleaded poverty, he repeatedly promised that I need bring nothing, that he'd look after me, pay for everything. I knew he was no oil sheikh, so I protested, I couldn't possibly . . .

"You don't understand. I'm very good with tourists, I have more money than you think and I've nothing to spend it on. All you need is a ticket."

Months of reassurances and pleading wore down my thin excuses. I shifted between thinking that my reluctance was common sense and worrying that it might be racism. What if he'd been French, American, something familiar? I didn't want to turn down the adventure for the wrong reasons, so I raided the scraps at the bottom of my bank account and pawned the gold jewellery I had from better times. The only ticket I could afford meant I had to stay in Jordan a fortnight. I bought it and left

25

London with just over sixty pounds in spare cash, heading for what my friends and relatives were convinced would be the end of me.

"I just know he's not an axe-murderer," I told my sister. She suggested that axe-murderers were relatively rare, but that stories of girls who'd had drugs put in their baggage by seemingly charming Arab consorts weren't so unusual. I promised not to leave him alone with so much as a tube of toothpaste belonging to me. That had been a friend's alarm-story: "You won't know if he plants Semtex on you. You can get enough Semtex to blow up a plane into a tube of toothpaste."

Since this particular friend was a librarian in a quiet country town who'd never been further than Boulogne, I felt inclined to doubt her expertise on terrorists and their methods with explosives. I told her she watched too much television. As I boarded the plane with a rising sense of panic, I told myself *I* watched too much television.

I sat waiting for takeoff, reading a collection of Philip K. Dick's short stories; it seemed full of tales of people who leave their house in a perfectly normal fashion one morning, only to find themselves transported into a parallel universe.

No perturbing sign of time running light years faster when I arrived in Paris to change planes. In the wait between flights I contemplated my guidebook, trying to work out exactly how possible it would be for a person of fairly wimpish disposition to survive a fortnight on sixty pounds – just in case Rathwan was waiting to greet me with an axe or an oddly bulging tube of toothpaste. Jordan wasn't cheap. The airport tax alone . . . I stopped myself and went to look for my next flight.

The desk that corresponded to my flight number seemed to be processing a flight to Beirut. I explained my problem to a curt man from Air France.

"Yes, yes. This is the flight to Amman."

"But it says Beirut."

"Beirut first, then Amman."

"Why doesn't it say Amman?"

"Because it is mainly for Beirut."

Perhaps flights to Beirut had to go in disguise. Had the way I'd asked for a ticket to Amman inadvertently been a code that told my travel agent I really meant Beirut? "Change in Paris, then straight on to Amman" – that was all she'd said. But had she winked at me oddly while she said it? How did people in London who wanted to go to Beirut know that there was a flight there if it didn't reveal itself until Paris? Maybe someone from Air France just phoned round the Lebanese community: "We're thinking of doing Beirut on Thursday. If enough of you are up for it, we'll re-route something." Or had the entire Air France organisation been hijacked that very morning?

The flight was packed. Were all the passengers relatives of the hijackers?

I sat next to a young French engineer who was going to Amman. Or thought he was. He was round, aftershave-soaked and highly pompous about all the travelling he got to do in his job. He asked me several questions about Jordan; I was polite for a while but began to distance myself when he asked me why I was going there.

"To visit friends."

"Oh good, I don't know anyone there. Do you know if there are any nightclubs in Amman? Perhaps we could meet up."

"I don't like nightclubs much."

"What about restaurants?"

"I don't really go to restaurants either."

"Surely you have to eat?"

"Not necessarily."

He laughed. "You're making fun of me. At least tell me how to get in touch with you."

I picked up my Philip K. Dick with a scowl.

"I'm afraid I can't tell you that." He didn't understand; I was going to a parallel universe.

I almost hooted with excitement as we came into Beirut. (I held myself in check because the engineer had already classified me as something too odd to talk to and might press the alarm to get me medical attention if I displayed one more twitch of oddness.) Everyone seemed to be leaving the plane. For a moment I thought the Air France man had been truly spiteful and the flight ended here after all. Then the steward told us that we'd be refuelling for an hour; passengers continuing to Amman could stretch their legs but weren't to leave the plane.

Excitement soared up in me again. Beirut. The trees really were the cedars of Lebanon, there really was a burnt-out, rusting tank by the runway. I expected the plane to be surrounded by snarling armed militia of some sort but there was only one vaguely uniformed man in sight, ceaselessly sauntering near the plane with a machine gun over his shoulder and his attention on his fingernails. Well, it must be a nightmare to be caught in a shoot-out with a bad manicure.

I moved around the plane, peering out of windows and doors. What I could see of the city's cream skyscrapers looked abandoned, as if they'd been left to rot and fall down rather than having been bombed or shelled. The airport building was from a 1950s film, again with an air of neglect: grass grew from the roof and sprouted through cracks in the old-fashioned concrete of the runway. Little trailers trundled out over the concrete to unload the cargo – cardboard boxes full of fresh flowers. They seemed sadly appropriate for Lebanon.

Amman's Queen Alia International Airport was bright, garish, modern, a '70s disco film set leaping with so many busy, lurid orange-suited cleaners they almost had to clean each other for something to do. I don't know what became of the engineer – hid till he saw I'd gone, I expect. I felt very vulnerable, convinced that one of the dozens of idling airline officials or soldiers would pounce on me and harangue me just to pass the time, before refusing to let me in to the country for having such a foolish reason for being there. No sign of Rathwan. That was it then: death, imprisonment, starvation . . . Then, smiling nervously, he was beside me.

At first I saw a total stranger. But as I sat with him in the airport buffet drinking tea, I once again saw the warm smile, the mile-long eyelashes; I heard the gentle compelling voice and felt everything would be all right.

He was amazed I was there at all, treated me as if I was so

fragile I was not quite real. Gradually, he began to relax and believe it. He laughed as he listened to my Beirut saga.

"And you know, you're right, it is mysterious. According to the newspaper, this plane was to come direct from Paris. Are you sure you weren't hijacked?"

He'd organised a taxi and booked a hotel for me. From the start I liked the Hotel Wadi, with its lounge full of guests who reacted to any newcomer as if they were in a private house: it would be unthinkable not to greet the stranger, offer tea, enquire about their welfare – we were all sharing a home.

Rathwan and I had dinner in the restaurant where we'd had our first meal together – the vines, fountains, lanterns were all the same, but our conversation was stilted now. I wasn't comfortable. Stuttering with embarrassment, I explained my financial predicament. He looked hurt.

"So, you don't trust me."

"What do you mean?"

"I told you there was no need to bring anything."

"I know, but you must think I'm mad to really not bring anything. I think I am."

"What's mad? You made sacrifices to buy your ticket, now I can pay to make it up to you. Please, the subject is finished, there's nothing to worry about."

Back at the hotel, we had rooms on separate floors. Islam doesn't have a lax attitude to unmarried couples. But in Rathwan's restrained parting handshake there seemed as much of his own caution as concern with religious strictures.

"In the morning I will meet you in the lounge at nine o'clock and we will plan our day. No one will disturb you. They are nice people in this hotel, don't worry about anything."

I fell asleep almost instantly, at peace. There were nice people around me in the hotel and an extremely nice man was emerging from the stranger at the airport.

Pillow-dwelling demons must have stolen away my peace of mind in the night. I was in the lounge by eight the next morning. I enquired after Rathwan at five to nine.

"*Barra.*" Amjad said. I didn't know this meant 'outside', but at my confused look Amjad pointed out of the window. Rathwan had gone? I breathed deeply. Perhaps he'd just stepped out for cigarettes, a morning constitutional . . . Or perhaps he'd gone off me and run screaming into the remotest corner of the desert.

By ten I was ready to go to the British Embassy and declare myself an insane person in need of immediate shipping home. Then he came in, grinning, joking with the staff – everyone knew Rathwan.

He apologised. "I went to find my friend. He has lent us a car for a few days, so we can go anywhere you'd like to go. But he talks too much and I had to listen for a long time. Let's go somewhere nice for some breakfast. Did you smoke all these?"

So I should have known, as I watched the snow fall on the dark streets of Amman three years later, that Rathwan never let me down. All the same, the fear of abandonment was creeping through me. A man who looked Saudi Arabian came into the lounge. I had learnt something in three years then – I could guess, from their features and style of dress, at the likely origin of the

31

different Arab nationals who flowed through the hotel.

The Saudi saw me and did a double take. I nodded a greeting to him and continued watching the snow.

"Merry Christmas," he said in English, and I nearly burst into tears.

Omar still hadn't returned to his post at the reception desk. Perhaps he was praying; Omar did a lot of praying in the back office. Sylvester Stallone seemed to have dozed off while remaining deceptively upright in his chair. Amjad braved out of his kitchen and managed to watch television for a few moments before the Saudi sent him for tea, for both of us. I declined but the Saudi insisted. The tea organised, Amjad risked another television break, poised on the edge of his seat as the respite was bound not to last long.

They were showing my favourite Jordanian programme, a melodramatic family saga about Bedouin – girls who didn't want to marry the men their fathers chose, financial skulduggery, evil stepmothers – a sort of *Dynasty* in tents, a goat opera. Six months had passed since I'd last watched it and the same lead girl was still flinging herself down on her mattress weeping, the same stepmother was still glinting her eyes wickedly at the camera . . .

It was getting late; I'd have to tear myself away from the excitement and do something practical. Like finding a mattress to fling myself on, weeping. Rather than wander aimlessly in the snow, I could probably get Omar to phone around and find me another hotel. If I could find Omar.

"*Wain* Omar?" I asked Amjad.

"*Barra*," he said. Well, that wasn't like Omar. For a strapping lad who couldn't have been more than twenty if he was a day, Omar always seemed content to devote his simmering energies to his reception desk and his prayers. Outside just wasn't the place for him to be. Amjad started to say something else when the door opened and Omar bounced in, grinning gleefully.

"Man!" he said, in his voice that never seemed quite broken. "Rathwan!"

There he was, all of a do, brushing snow out of his hair.

"I was at the post office, would you believe that? I was telephoning you. I thought you were coming tomorrow. You said the day before Christmas Eve."

"This *is* the day before Christmas Eve."

"No! So what's today called?"

"Nothing."

"Oh, it's too complicated. I'm glad I'm a Muslim," he laughed, and threw himself into the chair beside me. The Saudi watched him with undisguised irritation. Rathwan just got louder.

"Omar has been asking everyone in Amman where I am. He finds me on the telephone to you and tells me you're here. And I was worried that you didn't answer your phone. But you're here. Oh my poor sheep." ('Sheep' was a nickname I'd acquired thanks to my unruly shock of white-blonde hair and tendency to wander off on my own.) "Well, it's a terrible thing for a Bedouin to lose a sheep, but I'm happy now."

Omar was behind his reception desk once more, smiling to himself. Surely another point chalked up in heaven to add to his prayers. But then he spoke, and the angels hovered with erasers at the ready.

"Rathwan," he said, "*maa fii* rooms."

Rathwan gave him a look of incredulity and said something cheery in Arabic. Then he talked rapidly to the Saudi, charming him from irritation to affability in seconds.

"Everything is arranged. This man will share with his friend and you will take his room."

Rathwan then arranged a room for himself, 'with the boys'. This meant the tiny room by the back office where Omar, Amjad and Sylvester slept shoulder to shoulder on thin mattresses. To make space for the extra shoulders, Omar would sleep on the office couch. I said it wasn't fair to shift everyone around because of me. Perhaps we should go somewhere else.

Rathwan was having none of that. "Of course it's fair. You are a good customer, Omar should have organised something."

I felt that after his mercy dash out into the snow in his shirtsleeves, Omar deserved no criticism ever again in his life. Besides, very few of us average Joes and Omars had Rathwan's ability to charm people into instantly inconveniencing themselves.

Rathwan's busy mind had moved on.

"I have a Lebanese friend, a Christian, who has a restaurant. I have organised for us to have Christmas dinner there. Is that tomorrow?"

"The day after. Christmas Day."

"Oh. So there's an Eve and a Day, but they're not on the same day?"

"That's right. Then Boxing Day comes after that."

"Who?"

"Boxing Day."

"I've never heard of it. Are you making things up now? I'll tell you what will be much easier – change your religion. And then I can sell your present."

That gave us the full, choking, spluttering, unstoppable giggles. Omar, Amjad and Sylvester started laughing for no apparent reason except to keep us company; even the Saudi joined in, as if he might as well show willing for now and hope for an explanation later. I felt I'd come home for Christmas.

CHAPTER 2

No Story with a Girl

"I must ask you to keep out of the desert. This car is only for road driving."

Eggs had more tread than the Datsun's tyres. Its owner had his arm in a sling. He'd had an accident.

"Not in my car, of course. In stairs."

Of course.

I tried not to get too curious about the bedraggled nest of wires hanging down under the dashboard and thanked Rathwan's friend for the loan of the car.

"No problem. As you see, I have my accident."

The gears were stiff but the brakes seemed to work; I expected we'd survive his generosity if I could keep my feet out of the wires and aim for a top speed of ten miles an hour.

With a yell of delight, Rathwan found the car stereo in the glove compartment and began 'entertaining' me with tapes of very loud Bedouin songs. It was my very first day with him, but my lack of familiarity with Arab music overcame any getting-to-know-you politeness and I turned the songs off pretty sharpish. Their jaunty yelping was too much for nerves already precariously stretched by the no-indicating, minimal-bothering-to-look style of Jordanian driving. Rathwan infuriated me further by repeatedly leaning over and pressing the horn.

"Do you want to drive?"

"I don't have a licence."

"Then leave the horn alone."

"I don't need a licence for the horn."

He pressed it again.

"Stop that! Just leave it!"

All over the world, there's one thing men and women always fight over: if she's driving, he *can't* just leave it.

Rathwan reacted with irritating good humour to being screamed at: "But you drive too well for Jordan. You indicate. This means nothing to them, they only understand the horn."

I banged on the horn as a car pulled out of nowhere right in front of me.

"That's it," Rathwan laughed.

"I wish this was your face," I muttered and banged the horn again.

He looked at me, surprised. "Really? You have a bad temper like this?"

"No I haven't."

He grinned. "I like it. It's interesting. A new thing about you."

The road out of Amman was slaughterous with cars, lorries full of sheep, buses, jaywalkers and street-sellers pushing handcarts. Rathwan shopped out of the passenger window, buying oranges, bottled water and sandwiches from cartmen.

"Look, delicious." He waved sandwiches at me. Felafel chopped through with salad and fresh coriander, rolled in thin Arab bread – not delicious enough to stop me snapping ungraciously at his purchases:

"Don't show me sandwiches, we'll have an accident!"

Rathwan subsided temporarily, then said quietly to himself: "What made you crash the car? Well, officer, I was frightened by a sandwich."

The road eventually ran into the gravelly desert east of Amman. There were perhaps too many electricity pylons, factories and petrol stations along the road to call the scenery beautiful, but it reached clear to the blue horizon in a refreshing enough way after the swerving, stalling, U-turning, paint-scrape of the city. The only minor hassle with this wide open road was that it was the main trade route to Iraq – and in order to be an Iraqi truck driver, you need a particularly large truck and to think of driving as a blood sport; it's best not to shave too often either, so you look more scary. Points are scored according to the number of accident reports you can involve yourself in, but a real tournament winner is to get an oil tanker instead of a truck: fantastic-looking flames in a pile-up. Champions' technique is to pull out wildly to overtake, just missing an oncoming tanker before slamming back sharply into your lane, inches in front of a terrified foreign girl; brake a bit then too, so as to really shake her up. Or three of you can play together and box her in for a while so that she can't see if she's going to die in seconds or not.

Oh, the Iraqi lads know how to have fun on the road!

We passed a square, solid-looking castle on our right.

"We will go there later. My friend lives there."

"In a castle?"

Rathwan laughed. "Yes. That is the castle of Abu Hamdi. We will eat with him later. He's very special."

As if Abu Hamdi's castle signalled an edge to the city's furthest splash marks, the desert became emptier. Still not beautiful, the sort of desert people stagger around going mad in – all endlessly the same bleak, fawn scrub. Breathtaking, though, if you knew your way home.

The Omayyads didn't stagger around going mad out here – they thrived. Around the seventh century AD, they came out of the southern deserts of Arabia, battled the Byzantines out of power and made themselves an empire with Damascus as their capital. The remote castles they built or captured in the Jordanian desert were places they used for retreat from the refined civilisation they had created, places where they could ensure their old desert ways weren't forgotten. The Omayyads raced horses here, hunted game with falcons, saluki dogs and trained cheetahs. And while keeping a man in touch with his roots, the desert castles also doubled as havens of off-duty fun for the busy rulers, with music, dancing girls and luxury bathing facilities.

Time might have played a part in softening the appearance of Qusayr 'Amra against the sand, but the rounded domes and sinuous design of the building clearly intended it for gentle purposes. The ceilings and interior walls leapt with colourful frescoes of flowers, birds, hunting scenes and very unveiled ladies. There were pictures of the Omayyads' defeated enemies and their gods; those were the days when the Arabs lived Islam as a conquering, exploring creed, all confidence and curiosity. Painted on the inside of one of the domes over the bathing area was a map of the heavens showing stars in zodiacal constellations – space, not as we know it, but according to the scientists of the day. Tired out from the strains of empire-keeping and enemy-thrashing, an Omayyad caliph could soak and steam in his bath while looking up at the nobler fruits of his efforts: the art and learning that benefited from his patronage.

The yellow-brown bricks of Qusayr 'Amra melted invisibly into the sand as Rathwan and I wandered away into the surrounding desert. A few shady clumps of trees were the only indication that the wadi which ran by the castle wasn't permanently dried to dust. No sign of the birds and wild animals that the Omayyads chased about after – only the rolling desert and the heat-haze to watch.

As we watched, we abandoned talk of caliphs and Islamic civilisation and spoke of lesser things – ourselves. Rathwan had sixteen brothers and sisters. His father had married three wives.

"The first, my mother, is dead now. Since I was nineteen. But my father divorced her before that, when I was about seven. There were many problems. My mother was a very individual person but also she was sick."

The way he worded it made me think she must have been insane. But that wasn't it.

"Because she is sick she can have no more children than me and my two sisters. My father wanted many children. She is angry that he wants another wife. He divorced her and we came to the city, to live in a small house beside my mother's sister. It was very hard for my mother."

He told me this lightly, as if it had just occurred to him as a minor point of interest – nothing to the way I'd laid on my sob-stories. He was stronger than sadness.

"So you weren't brought up in the desert?"

"Not after that age, no. But I would visit my father. Sometimes. Now it's easier to visit him. We are trying to . . . come to terms. Visiting the desert with my friends is the best thing. I do love it. In the city I have a good job, I like to meet people from other cultures, learn about other ways of life. But eventually I will go back to the desert."

A light wistfulness drifted over us. I tried to lift it away.

"When is that? Eventually?"

"It is . . ." he smiled, "eventually."

Meanwhile there were more desert castles to see.

"Actually, the translation is wrong," he told me. "Foreigners call them desert 'castles' but *qasr* really means 'palace'."

Now that I knew this I felt most superior to foreigners. I shook my fist and hooted my horn at Iraqi truck drivers as if I was one of the boys.

Originally built by foreigners, Qasr al-Hallabat stood looking tough at the top of an incline. The only way we could reach it was by breaking our promises to the arm-accident friend and taking the car up a rocky cart track. The Romans had built the castle – palace – from heavy, grey basalt as a defence against marauding desert tribes, but got marauded out in the end. The

41

Omayyads took it over, adding more towers and twiddly bits, for their own defence purposes. And, of course, for a spot of hunting and recreation.

Rathwan explained the history to me – he had information about each palace scrolling through his head and a routine of special features to point out. All in a day's work.

"Now I expect you want to climb on everything," he said as he concluded this personalised tour.

"Climb on everything?"

"Foreigners like this. In all the ruins they don't feel they have seen the thing properly until they have climbed on it."

I wanted to shatter his generalisation; I didn't want to be a foreigner. (Particularly as he always said 'foreigner' with an air of affectionate amusement, the way people talk about kittens – not very bright but harmless; just don't let them get their funny little paws into anything important.) But I was bursting at my foreign seams to go clambering up some piles of ancient rubble, scale a few walls and stand on the highest point of the ruins. Rathwan, having no such foolish urges in his bloodline, leant against a rock and read his newspaper.

"I suppose you think I'm a typical foreigner now," I said when I came down from my conquest of the stones.

"No," he smiled, "you are not typical at all." Then he gave me a longer look. "You are more typical of a small boy, covered in dirt."

Indignantly, I checked myself in the wing mirror; yes, I'd definitely brought half the ruins back to the car on my clothes and my face.

"Never mind, the next place is an Omayyad baths."

It was a small bathhouse, Hammam as-Sarakh, and not exactly open for the passing wash-and-brush-up trade. Only a few splashes of coloured plaster suggested it was once as prettily decorated as Qusayr 'Amra. Small standing columns exposed below floor level showed that the baths had been heated by lighting fires underneath them, and a ribbed dome gave a sense of a once-elegant construction; otherwise the remains of the bathhouse and attached living quarters were in ant-crawled bits. I felt sorry for the little place standing neglected and un-signposted at the end of a winding gravel track. I liked its name, imagining that Sara was the favourite mistress of one of the caliphs, that she had lived here in lonely luxury, waiting for her prince to arrive.

"Do you think so?" Rathwan looked dubious. "Actually, *sarakh* means 'desert'. The name means 'desert baths'. There's no story with a girl."

After a particularly close scrape with an Iraqi oil tanker and death, I was more than happy to stop sightseeing for the day. When we pulled into Azraq Rest House to find a restaurant with pot plants and marble floors, and little, tree-shaded white cabins grouped round a swimming pool, I felt it was no more than I deserved. Each cabin had a small terrace with roses growing round the porch supports and aromatic greenery in window boxes. I had a hot shower and thought, "Actually, 'cabin' is the wrong translation. 'Palace' would be better."

The head waiter, Achmad, was a friend of Rathwan's. He

served us coffee by the pool, gossiped with Rathwan for a few minutes and then asked if we'd be having dinner at the rest house.

"No," said Rathwan, "I think we will have dinner with Abu Hamdi." Achmad laughed at the very mention of the name.

That evening I got myself dressed up a bit, as was only fitting for a dinner guest at a castle. So I was surprised by the nature of the 'gifts' that Rathwan made us stop to buy for the King of the Castle – onions, tomatoes, tea, bread and sugar. Perhaps this king had fallen on hard times.

I was even more surprised at the sight of a vast, wedding-cake extravaganza of a hotel on the outskirts of Azraq; why did they need this, out here in the middle of nowhere, when the rest house half a mile away was almost empty? It struck me that there was something very odd about Azraq town.

"Actually," Rathwan explained, "it is *two* towns."

To the left of the cross-roads in Azraq was a peaceful town of polite but taciturn people: Druze, who had fled to Jordan from Syria decades before. Conservative, religious, secretive, they quietly kept shops in genteel poverty. To the right of the cross-roads, however, was a blaze of lights and a blare of music from dozens of little restaurants and gaudy shops.

"You will find it like this all night," Rathwan said disapprovingly.

The right-hand town was scruffy, heaving with life and neon like a cheap seaside resort. But the cars were new and flashy – Cadillacs, Mercedes, a Daimler, swarms of the sort of cute, pricey little sports cars an Iraqi truck would eat for breakfast . . . What was going on?

Right-hand Azraq was full of Saudis who didn't live there. Right-hand Azraq was really a Chechen town, settled by refugees who'd arrived the last time the Russians took against their people. The Chechens had got a fine trade going for themselves: alcohol. Azraq was a mere thirty miles from the border with 'dry' Saudi Arabia, and every little restaurant in the right-hand town had a back-room drinking parlour, every little shop an under-the-counter off-licence. The posh wedding-cake hotel had been built to help accommodate all the Saudis fleeing across the desert for a night of fun.

Fleeing across the desert to Abu Hamdi, I watched out for drivers of flash cars who might not be seeing straight, as well as for truck drivers who didn't think straight – or, worst of all, a truck driver who'd been frequenting the Chechen speakeasies.

Abu Hamdi's Qasr al-Kharanah was the only castle in the Eastern Desert the Omayyads built purely for defence. No baths, no dancing, no messing about. We pulled up at the gate in the wire perimeter fence and Rathwan pressed the horn. So: soon I was to join the circle of those who knew why to laugh affectionately at the very mention of Abu Hamdi; the only information I'd been allowed en route was that he was Rathwan's cousin.

I noticed a small concrete building several hundred yards behind the castle; a Bedouin came to the door, went back in and re-emerged with a big stick. He began walking towards us, brandishing his stick: a large, round man of about fifty, his Bedouin dress all of a flap, his *kefiyah* roped to his head at an eccentric angle. He was shouting something with every flourish of his stick.

45

"He wants us to leave the car and walk. Cars are not allowed in, but it will be all right for us."

Rathwan got out, and the round, flapping man stopped in his tracks. Then he rushed at us, waving his stick violently and roaring what seemed to be terrible oaths. When he got to the gate, he reached over it to strike at Rathwan with the stick. Rathwan yelped and jumped back. The man laughed delightedly and opened the gate.

"So you see, this is Abu Hamdi," Rathwan grinned.

Abu Hamdi locked the gate behind us and climbed into the back of the car, upbraiding Rathwan loudly, jumping up and down on the seat and complaining about it; the seat springs complained back.

"He says this must be my car – it is rubbish."

The small building, rather than the castle, was where Abu Hamdi really lived. Two rooms: one with a tiny Calor Gas stove and elementary cooking utensils; the other, the more proudly kept main room of the house, containing a single bed made with hospital precision, a neat pile of cardboard boxes on a battered suitcase, a highly decorated *narjileh* pipe, a couple of termite-eaten armchairs and a chipped, wooden coffee table with small possessions laid out on it in carefully considered order, like objects put out on a tray for a children's memory game – razor, soap, tobacco, lighter, a cracked fragment of mirror, a key, a German coin and a comb.

At the front of the house was a concrete patio with a border of soil. Here Abu Hamdi had struggled to make a garden: geraniums and roses, gasping in the summer heat. Optimistically, he'd built a complex wire trellis that arched up to meet his roof at one end of the patio; but the roses just leant against the foot of it feebly, whimpering.

Even with an almost complete language barrier, I could see how funny Abu Hamdi was. He reminded me of W.C. Fields, both in his bearing and his tone of voice, although his dark skin was considerably less lived-in than W.C.'s – unlined and health-ily clear. From time to time, a broad smile would dispel his air of studied ferocity; then, remembering himself, he'd mutter darkly and scowl again.

"He says the gifts are rubbish. Why didn't I bring him some meat instead of this goat food?"

Nevertheless, Abu Hamdi grumbled the gifts into his lair and put on a kettle for tea.

"Sit, Madame." He pulled a chair out to the centre of the room, indicating expansively that this was the best position as I'd have a view of the castle through the door. Then, "Rathwan!" he growled, and pointed to the ground outside. To extend the joke, Rathwan went outside – then rebelled, coming back in with a wicked grin while Abu Hamdi shooed at him.

"I will ask him why he's not receiving us in his castle."

An outburst of Arabic and loud laughter.

"Abu Hamdi says he's sorry, but this is his summer hunting lodge. He only uses his main castle in winter but he will show you round later."

In describing Qasr al-Kharanah, one of my guidebooks said: 'The affable Bedouin caretaker will come out of his hut and show you round'. Abu Hamdi would have set up a huge complaint at

47

such a description. For one thing, he was the castle *guard*, the only thing that stood between the castle and its annihilation by marauders, misbehaving tourists or whoever else might lay siege to it. And his so-called 'hut' was the home he lived in six days a week, alone with his thoughts and his housework. In another guidebook I was startled to see a picture of Abu Hamdi captioned 'A typical Bedouin'. If Abu Hamdi was typical, *Lawrence of Arabia* would have been a knockabout comedy with Turks losing their trousers, Bedouin chasing them off the playing fields of Arabia with hockey sticks, and the British in the officers' mess playing poker for Jerusalem.

Having been miscast in life and robbed of the star roles he should have had in comedy films, Abu Hamdi was delighted to have any sort of audience. He made a great show of his incessant Rathwan-tormenting: moving him from wherever he sat and dusting the place afterwards while pulling disgusted faces, handing me a glass of sweet, strong tea and pretending he didn't know Rathwan was there at all.

"I asked him what has happened to my tea. He asks if you can hear another man's voice in the room or is there a ghost?"

Rathwan did without tea, dozing off when he was finally allowed to settle on the bed. After we'd communed silently for a while, Abu Hamdi began telling me something about Rathwan. I heard the word *kaslaan* several times. I got out my dictionary. Abu Hamdi tapped it encouragingly: "Yes, good, yes." *Kaslaan* – lazy. I nodded energetically.

Next, Abu Hamdi mimed throwing water on Rathwan; then he pretended to set fire to him, to crush his head with a stone and, finally, to stab him with a sharp Bedouin knife. When Rathwan woke with a start, perhaps from some frightening dream of being attacked with a knife, Abu Hamdi and I were sitting primly in dignified silence.

"What's going on?"

"Nothing." A giggle started to well out of me.

"You are sitting suspiciously. Why are you smiling?"

"I can't smile?"

"Not if you're up to some trick with Abu Hamdi. I know him, he was doing something. Japes."

"Japes?"

"I have used the correct word?"

"It's the correct word, but he was doing nothing."

Rathwan pulled a hard-done-by face. "Oh, this is terrible. Already you start to lie to me."

Abu Hamdi put an end to the japes by picking up his stick, adjusting his headgear still further off-centre and assuming his role as castle guard.

Qasr al-Kharanah had only one outer door, but there were legions of arrow slits in its arm-thick walls. On either side of the vaulted entrance to the central courtyard were long, high rooms that had once been stables. Steps led up from the courtyard to smaller rooms decorated with carved plaster: the living quarters. Abu Hamdi tapped his stick at the carvings: "See good." He then charged us through to the next room, tapping more carvings as he went: "See good." Occasionally, he would swing his stick at an arrow slit: "See shoot." When we returned to the entrance, he pointed to some inscribed stones, supposedly incorporated from an earlier structure: "See Greeks." The lightning tour ended with a theatrical bow, accompanied by a drum-majorette toss of his stick: "See finish."

Back at his summer residence, Abu Hamdi began to prepare dinner. I offered to help but Rathwan decided that I'd done my work for the day by driving; he would help Abu Hamdi.

"I'll enjoy it. I can annoy him. You can be waited on like a princess."

A stone bench covered in cushions ran along the outer wall of the little house; I stretched out on it, definitely feeling quite princessy with the scent of the struggling roses around me. The sun was going down and the traffic on the road was beginning to thin away to nothing. I could hear Abu Hamdi and Rathwan laughing and taunting each other between quiet bouts of vegetable chopping.

On one Calor Gas ring they made a surprisingly flavourful stew of potatoes, onions and tomatoes, into which we dipped flaps of bread. Abu Hamdi wanted me to know the food would have been much nicer if Rathwan hadn't poisoned it with his interference.

Afterwards, when we went out to have tea on the terrace, the road was silent. Apart from our little house on the prairie, there was nothing for miles. Our only light was an old hurricane lamp which made shadow monsters of the roses; the hiss of the kettle in Abu Hamdi's kitchen the only sound. I felt as though we should talk in whispers, but Rathwan and Abu Hamdi roared at each other in the usual way, as if they were in the middle of a busy market.

"I'm sorry," Rathwan interrupted himself. When he spoke English, he almost whispered; I wondered if perhaps Arabic didn't work below a certain decibel level. "We are talking of family matters – not very interesting, but he wants to know the news."

Abu Hamdi seemed to get the gist of this and turned to me with an exaggerated yawn, shaking his head. "Rathwan no," he said, then smiled and indicated that I should speak. "Madame yes."

He made yet more tea, brought out an armchair and settled himself into it. Burbling on his *narjileh* pipe and beaming drowsily at his silhouetted garden, he looked like a contented sultan; he even had an occasional wise word for his subjects – "Madame good, Rathwan no."

After half an hour or so he began talking to Rathwan in unusually quiet Arabic. A more serious Abu Hamdi now, contemplative.

"He's telling me about some Dutch tourists who came this morning. He says he likes the foreigners. He likes the way of the foreigners. They have their freedom. The Arabs have very limited thinking."

Liberal sensibilities perturbed, I said that the Arabs had started many of the world's great thoughts.

"Oh yes," Rathwan sighed. "We know this. But we wonder if we have continued."

It was getting late. We promised to come back soon as we were hugged together in one huge Abu Hamdi farewell embrace.

Now comes something I'm half inclined not to write about.

Partly because it's obvious, partly because it's nobody's business but Rathwan's and mine. More importantly, I'm wary of exacerbating the problems Western women might encounter when travelling in the Middle East. In the Arab world, foreign girls, as we're called (this means particularly white Northern Europeans, North Americans or Australians), are often assumed to be easy sexual prey and to exert a malign, corrupting influence on local morality. My own assumption – that I'm entitled to freedom of choice in affairs of the heart – is all I have for an argument in the face of this generalisation. Of course it's an argument that means nothing to the sort of Arab men – they're usually men – making the generalisation. But are they likely to read this book? About as likely as the sort of Westerner who thinks that people should stick to their own race and kind, and must have something wrong with them if they don't. Anyway, I need to tell the truth about what happened, which means I can't leave stuff out to make allowances for the possible limited thinking of possible readers. So I'll tell it.

Of course Rathwan and I became more than 'just good friends'. It wasn't easy. He had a two-room apartment in Amman, rented from a nosy landlord; there would have been no question of my being seen within fifty feet of these bachelor quarters. We stayed in hotels, preferably run by people who knew Rathwan; or, rather, by people whom he knew weren't going to creep around at night and spy on us. We always took separate rooms; if we became unseparated in the course of the night, we were always back where we should be by morning calls. We had the vast, romantic privacy of the desert. We had the benefit of a brain cell or two between us and we practised discretion to the point of paranoia. It grew less and less easy with time, as the bond between us deepened; we were both sensitive creatures, we didn't want our relationship pushed into any corners where it would become, or seem to become, squalid.

Now that you know, I won't mention it again – but I thought I'd better tell you. It was so much a part of what we had to deal with. You can't just go off to the desert and have an affair. Unless you're rich. Then you can move to the more Westernised areas of cities, areas less bound together by tradition and gossiping neighbourliness. In the deserts or Downtown, in the world that Rathwan inhabited, we were breaking the law. As I was a foreigner, there'd probably just have been an extremely embarrassing scene if we'd been discovered; in more remote areas, I might have had a few stones thrown at me. Had I been a local girl, Rathwan could have faced a few months in prison. Had I been a local girl, I could have joined the girls in Jordanian prisons who never want to leave; the prison sentences they incur for misdemeanours with men they're not married to are nothing to what they could face from their families. A newspaper report of a girl hacked to death by her brother who 'suspected' she'd been fornicating was nothing unusual; nor was the refusal of her family to press charges as it was 'a private matter'.

Although hacking and imprisonment might not have been on the cards for us, learning more about Jordanian culture eventually helped me understand why Rathwan feared trouble from the start. Having an affair with a foreign woman wasn't as bad as being caught murdering someone (especially if it was just your sister) but it brought the same level of shame as being branded a thief in Western society. Perhaps if I'd known more at the beginning, I'd have wondered if I wanted to begin at all.

Back at the rest house in Azraq, we had a cup of coffee by the deserted poolside, stars and fairy lights reflecting on the water. Two Saudis scuttled furtively to a cabin carrying brown paper bags that clinked. Chechen shopping. Rathwan didn't look at them – he was watching me very carefully.

"I'm so happy you're here," he said.

"I think I like it here."

"Really, this has been such a good day."

"Yes."

"I'm afraid to spoil anything." He paused. "I'm afraid to be wrong in what I say because I want every day to be like this, with no bad feeling."

"Why would that happen?"

He went silent, staring at the water. Suddenly, he had a rush of courage: "You know, I think there is a cockroach in my cabin."

He looked at me steadily, but on the verge of flight around his edges.

"There isn't one in mine."

He smiled, edges resting. "I was hoping you would say that."

There, it was done.

Apart from the Saudis, everyone was back where they should be at eight the following morning. The Saudis were comatose on their terrace, with three empty bottles on the table in front of them: whisky, vodka and Cinzano. No ice, no mixers – the shortest route to oblivion.

The sun was already searing and the pool was calling just for me.

"Why would I? I'm a Bedouin from the desert," was Rathwan's logical reason for seeing no point at all in swimming.

We had a slow breakfast, Rathwan fussing that my hair was still wet, that I'd get pneumonia and probably die just when he'd found me. To ward off a fatal chill I sunbathed while he read a newspaper. After an hour or so, Rathwan worried that having escaped pneumonia I would now burn myself in the mad dog sun.

"I see it all the time: foreigners, bright red and sick."

As I'd fully intended to sunbathe until I was bright red and sick, I pretended I was doing no such embarrassing thing and was simply desperate to get back to castle sightseeing.

As we were saying goodbye to Achmad, I noticed one of the Saudis staggering dangerously close to the pool; I couldn't tell if he was merely confused or contemplating suicide. Well, I'd have been depressed if his night on the terrace was my idea of fun. It might be kind if the Chechens were to add to their enterprises with a counselling centre or perhaps just a liver-transplant clinic.

At Qasr al-Azraq, a very old guard showed me photos of his father with Lawrence of Arabia; he also showed me the grim, black basalt room above the gatehouse where Lawrence had slept. Omayyads had been there before him, Romans before them. The massive stone doors and the great dark slabs of the basalt walls must have looked reassuringly secure to Lawrence, as he set up headquarters in the castle for the final stages of the Arab Revolt against the Turks.

Rathwan thought Lawrence had been extremely brave; I thought he might well have been brave but that he wasn't very bright.

Rathwan looked offended. "I don't think all those Arabs would have followed an idiot."

"I don't mean he was an idiot. I mean he wasn't clever enough to match the politicians."

"Oh well, politicians."

"They made him look like an idiot."

"They made him look like a liar. It wasn't his fault. That's what I heard. And the Turks are gone. The Bedouin like him."

Of course they do. What a PR job for their lifestyle.

Down in the seaside town of Aqaba, my Australian friends and I had met many a friendly shopkeeper who'd told us his father had been an extra in the film; so many that we started to doubt the lot of them – until the photo albums came out and there indeed was Dad with Omar Sharif and the boys. A great way to keep customers interested. Especially if you could then produce a picture of a grandfather who took part in the real thing.

The Bedouin of southern Jordan who make a living taking tourists through Wadi Rum to show them where Lawrence did what (with a lot of poetic licence) are as much indebted to him for what he wrote as what he did. Lawrence told the West that all Bedouin are the embodiment of courage, hospitality, loyalty and near-superhuman endurance. In fact, what the Jordanian Bedouin know they're selling tourists is the thrill of talking to a real Bedouin about Lawrence – never mind the famous man himself. You can't buy a 'Lawrence of Arabia' T-shirt, an 'I went where T.E. did' sticker or an Aircraftman Shaw memorial motorbike; but you *can* buy wall-to-wall Bedouin memorabilia – knives, rugs, clothes, coffee pots . . . The very first thing I heard Rathwan say was "My name is Rathwan, I am a Bedouin, I come from the desert." He knew full well the effect that this little introduction would have on foreigners: "Hello, I'm a walking legend, follow me."

While looking like he was leading the Bedouin, Lawrence was actually following, copying and aggrandising them. Many English writers and travellers have done the same. I'm inclined to find it all a bit patronising and tinted like portraits of Noble Savages. Why would the Bedouin be born more courageous, loyal, or whatever than the rest of us? Of course there were special individuals among them, but special individuals are found scattered all over the earth. Circumstances shape people's behaviour, customs and ability to endure, that's all.

I daresay Lawrence might find the likes of Rathwan and Abu Hamdi extremely debased creatures – not enduring or fighting half as much as their ancestors. Yet their heritage lay just below the surface, adapted to modern times but very much alive. Wasn't guiding tourists a version of the work Bedouin had always done, acting as escorts through the desert? Although their adventures might seem tamer than the Boys' Own mythology invented around their ancestors, the Bedouin world was still one in which men went larking about together in the desert and women didn't figure in the story.

Driving back into Amman from our days of desert adventure, I wondered if it was going to be like this the whole time I was with Rathwan: no sign of another woman, just me moving in his male domain, yet another Westerner who'd only ever know the Boys' Own part of Bedouin culture.

Before we checked ourselves back into the Hotel Wadi, forty thousand male passers-by guided me into a parking space on the busy street, volunteering themselves for the job in that completely unhelpful way of men world-wide – waving, shouting, banging the back of the car, getting in the space the driver needs to manoeuvre into and generally assuming that a woman will make a tomato stew of things unless they assist her through the ordeal.

While I had a shower and calmed down from my parking rage, Rathwan had been out investigating a rumour he'd heard of a Palestinian concert that was to be held in the Roman theatre that evening – a rare event, well worth seeing. He returned with the news that the concert was definitely on. In the way he did such things, he had a free ticket for me, and cigarettes as well – he'd noticed me smoke my last one down to my elbow after the parking incident.

As we headed off for the concert, we ran into a gang of noisy men coming out of a cinema in a crowded Downtown alley. You'd hardly notice the cinema was there at all: its narrow, grubby frontage was all but blocked off with market stalls. Only a sign saying 'Cinema' in sooty neon, with the initial 'C' burnt out, gave away the location.

"What film is on?"

"Rubbish," said Rathwan. "Only men go in these places, you wouldn't be interested."

"What sort of rubbish?"

"Foreign films. You know."

I immediately thought he must mean porn, which explained why the men had come out braying with excitement.

"What kind of foreign films?"

"You know, for men. Kung fu, Rambo, that kind of thing."

No story with a girl.

CHAPTER 3

Kings, Film Stars and the Boys

The Roman theatre was the hub of Amman. Fully restored, its six-thousand-seat amphitheatre was a sun trap by day and a romantically lit mystery by night. The ancient stones had seen emperors and gladiators; these days they were dotted with climbing foreigners, picnicking school groups, deeply conversing men or meekly hand-holding couples. It was a place for everyone – except boys.

Ismat, an elderly Palestinian, guarded the theatre. He was tiny, all concertina-ed in on himself like a little clay icon that had been left out to melt in the sun, and he decided who was allowed through the theatre's high metal gates. Foreigners were OK: they meant possible tips for him or for the tourist guides who hung around the small prefab house just inside the gates which served as Ismat's on-duty home. Grown-up Arabs, families and supervised children also passed muster with him, but boys . . .

Usually, Ismat was too alert to let his arch-enemies get

anywhere close to the theatre; if any boys (between six and twelve seemed to be the particularly offensive age) so much as lurked too near the gates, he'd rush up and bang a stick against the metal bars: "Boys get away from the gate! Boys get away!" But if Ismat had been dozing or distracted and boys had managed to sneak in, he would blow his whistle and bellow, dancing around the theatre floor in a frenzy until he was obeyed. The boys were usually doing no more harm than having races up the steps or sitting in the sun nattering; they could try ignoring Ismat, but the perfect acoustics transmitted his rage loud and clear to all corners of the theatre. Sometimes he looked like he'd explode into fragments if he was defeated by them, but that cataclysmic day hadn't arrived yet.

However, Ismat had rather hoist himself on his own obsession. I really don't imagine that an archaeological site was all that interesting to small boys, but the game of trying to slip past Ismat must have been passed down from brother to brother as a great way to kill a few hours after school.

Policemen and soldiers had replaced Ismat on the evening of the Palestinian concert. Rathwan was greeted boisterously by a pack of them who were guarding the gate.

"My friends," he told me. I noticed he didn't need a ticket.

The amphitheatre was packed. As we went in, I was filtered to the right to sit with the women and children; men and boys (lots of boys: Ismat was probably lying somewhere heavily sedated) were sent to the left. Husbands could sit with their wives, but by the looks of it most chose not to; the men's section was far more densely crowded than the women's.

Rathwan told me he would probably sit nowhere in particular. "There are friends here with the police who I haven't seen for years, so I will move around to talk with them. But I'll come back to you every few minutes."

I was perfectly happy, sitting in the early-evening sun at the end of one of the stone terraces, watching the huge crowd settle itself down. I was next to a big cheerful woman, her white robes panelled with the red and pink embroidery favoured by Palestinian women. Most of the audience were Palestinians, waiting to see one of their most famous singers. The atmosphere was sparking with excitement and a thousand conversations built together into a roar.

The security and segregation were extra strict. The night before there'd been trouble and several arrests. Some of the Palestinian men in the audience had got too riled up by the singer's rendition of overtly political numbers. He'd been asked to temper his repertoire this evening, but even so, the instant he began, riled up began all over again.

The singer was a portly, middle-aged man in a grey suit and red-and-white *kefiyah*. He scarcely moved when he sang, just occasionally lifted one hand out to his side in a mildly imploring gesture. In Europe he'd have been a Pavarotti – the power and tone of his voice reached right into you and shivered your timbers, until you wanted to shout or weep. What on tape had always sounded to me like the lingering wailing of Arabic song was suddenly understandable as music. The 'wails' were single, endlessly held notes. I could hear the quality, the shadings and strength of this man's voice as it filled the vast open air, rising through and away over the crowd.

A backing group played a mixture of traditional and modern instruments; at peak moments, they would sing along with the star. The songs seemed to follow similar patterns: slow, unaccompanied beginnings, speeding up as the percussion built insistently and swelling with the rhythmic clapping that spread through the spectators.

The men in the audience were losing their minds; it was like a cross between a football match and an evangelical rally. They were waving, screaming, weeping, ripping off their shirts, swaying up on their feet roaring. They were dancing in pairs on the narrow terraces, entwining provocatively with each other. Their dance was flashed through with images from other dances: the tango, flamenco . . . The dancers improvised around each other, their bodies very close together but never quite touching. Their feet barely moved; from time to time a stamp of the foot would send a quiver through the men, but the power of the dance lay in the sinuously swaying torsos, in the way the dancers would hold their arms quite still, high above their heads, for the space of long, smouldering encounters with each other.

Over on the women's side there was swaying, clapping and broad smiling – we were happy, but a long way from the men's hysteria. The woman next to me beamed warmly when she noticed I was tapping my feet. We bonded further when an officious suited man, wearing some sort of officious person's badge, tried to make her two teenage sons move from the step in front of her and go to the men's side. When she claimed responsibility for them, he fussed that they should sit up next to her; I moved along to make this possible. Mr Badge then wanted me to shift to the floor of the arena, where posh-looking people and a few foreigners occupied rows of plastic chairs.

At first I thought he was ordering me down there so I turned belligerent. "Why? I want to sit here. Why should I go down there?"

The Palestinian woman held me firmly by the arm and snapped at the man in Arabic. Looking hurt and bewildered, he said to me, "But the chairs are better." I belatedly realised that he thought a foreigner would be happier out of the cheap seats; he'd meant well by me.

Rathwan brought me a cold drink. He'd been worried I might be annoyed by his absence but I was having such a great time I'd barely thought about him.

"It's just that my friends are here, but they're on duty so I'm standing with them."

"I know, I'm fine. This woman is nice, everything's nice."

"Yes, you look happy. Good."

"I only wish I knew what they were singing about."

He sighed. "Oh, it's the usual with Palestinians. Their lost land, the usual."

A small boy was struggling up the steps with a copper kettle of tea, a sheaf of mint tucked into his belt and a bag of plastic cups strung over his shoulder. Rathwan bought some of his mint-garnished, over-sweetened tea. My new friend had been eavesdropping so closely, the boy thought she was with us and gave us three cups. I offered her the extra one; she refused at first, but took it when Rathwan urged her. She asked him a question.

"*Naam*," he said. Yes.

She looked at me with an approving nod.

"What did she ask you?"

"She asked if you are my wife."

When he left, she glanced admiringly at his back and then grinned at me as if to say 'lucky girl'.

Occasionally a shout went up way above the normal level of applause: the singer had started a house favourite. Small children from the front rows would pour down onto the floor of the theatre and perform strange, energetic dances behind the toffs in the plastic seats. After a nasty outbreak of tripping up and tears, policemen herded them back up to their mothers. At the start of the next big hit number the children came cavorting down again, and the policemen resigned themselves to the role of righting upturned toddlers and dabbing tears.

All too soon, the show was over. The women's side emptied quickly. Most of the men remained where they were, exhausted, staring at the empty stage with its huge backdrop – an enor- mously overblown photograph of King Hussein surrounded by Jordanian flags – their chance to yell and dance out years of anger all over. I didn't want it to end. I sat watching the female crowd flood down around me until Rathwan appeared, breaking my absorption in the moment:

"You'll be stood on."

He was hoping his policemen friends could get away in time to join us at the cafe opposite the theatre, but that would depend on 'the developments'.

From the raised terrace of the cafe I could see the Roman

theatre steps were emptying out, but a big crowd still surged around the gardens that separated the cafe from the theatre; policemen and soldiers stood in solid clumps throughout the surge, probably hoping they weren't in for 'developments'.

The roof-top cafe was part of a flash, multi-storey hotel that American and Lebanese businessmen had thrown up slap-bang in the middle of everyone's view. The authorities made them pull it down almost immediately, leaving only the ground-floor restaurant and shops; a sea of white tables occupied what had once been the first floor and was now the flat roof of their folly. Trees screened the cafe from the road on one side; the view of the public gardens and the theatre on the other side made it one of my favourite places to sit and watch the world go by. The air was always sweet with Turkish coffee and the aromatic tobacco smoked in six-foot-tall *narjileh* pipes made of brightly polished silver festooned with colourful tassels. Groups of young men would grandly order up the pipes to have with their coffee; they often looked comically self-conscious, sucking at the pipes as if the next puff would instantly bring the assured aura of manhood they desired. Waiters, wearing black satin Ottoman trousers, white puff-sleeved shirts, red cummerbunds and red fezzes, dashed from table to table serving customers with theatrical flourish. Sometimes they would charge terrifyingly along the length of the terrace swinging flat metal plates from long thin chains – plates piled with red-hot coals for the pipes; luckily they all seemed to have practised the wild swings enough to know how much gravity would save customers from a burning lapful.

Looking far too much like young Italian film stars than any

men in dark-blue uniforms and knee-length leather boots have a decent right to, two policeman were making their way to our table in a flash of white teeth and glint of glossy black hair. The kissing, backslapping and handshaking that went on between them and Rathwan suggested a lifelong separation rather than half an hour. Bashir and Salah couldn't join us – they had to stay on duty until two in the morning in case the Palestinians did anything untoward – but they'd wanted to say hello.

Salah, who was even better looking than his companion, was extremely serious and didn't speak English. Bashir was confidently inaccurate:

"I am lovely to meet you. Tomorrow we will meet much. We will eat dinners and meet much."

Adjusting their holsters, they went back to the Roman theatre after a loud, long parting exchange with Rathwan.

"These are my best friends. Salah is from my home village."

"They're Bedouin?"

"Yes, most soldiers and policemen are Bedouin. Because we're very brave."

"Of course."

"And because we are very patient with sarcasm from foreign girls."

Over coffee, I was bleating with excitement and praising the concert so much that Rathwan began to mutter about the high quality of Bedouin music – yes, when the Bedouin did a show that *was* something . . . Like many pure Jordanians, Rathwan could be ambivalent about Palestinians. Of course they were to be supported in their struggle. In theory. When I'd first met him, one of our tour group had mentioned going on from Jordan to visit Israel. Rathwan had looked at him coldly: "How can you visit a country that doesn't exist?"

Big talk. A great help I'm sure.

After a disastrous defeat by Israel in the Six Day War of 1967, Jordan had to give up its West Bank Territory, including its share of Jerusalem. Homeless Palestinians fled into Jordan, and subsequent guerrilla incursions from Jordan to Israel caused King Hussein to fear for the rest of his country should Israel make tough reprisals. In 1971, a civil war broke out when the king ordered the Jordanian army to quell Palestinian guerrilla activity; eventually the army drove the Palestinian activists out of Jordan.

However, King Hussein didn't give up his claim to the West Bank until 1988. There was more than stubborn pride involved in this stand. When Hussein was a boy, his grandfather, King Abdullah, was assassinated before his eyes by a Palestinian who'd been infuriated by Abdullah's willingness to negotiate with Zionists. King Hussein grew up knowing never to underestimate Palestinian rage, never to move from the political fence without looking very carefully at the ground on either side. He maintained martial law in Jordan until 1991 in order to prevent Palestinians fighting their cause from his territory; but he welcomed them if they wanted to live peaceably under his protection.

No Palestinians hold senior government or military posts in Jordan; they are a state within a state, guests who are subtly discriminated against and expected to be very tactful. Highly educated, hard-working, good at business, some Palestinians do better than native Jordanians. A lot of them don't; in this small country, the right Bedouin tribal connection is an important leg up the ladder.

Having been totally caught up in Rathwan's version of Jordan, I was shocked when I first heard the word 'Bedouin' used pejoratively. An affable Palestinian academic, in a job way below his level of qualification, complained to me: "The trouble with this country is it's run by Bedouin, you know, tribes, just out of tents. Merit means nothing, everything is in the power of these Bedouin."

He used the word the way we'd say 'Fascist' – no, less hatred than that, more contempt and bewildered despair; nothing to the way he said the word 'Israeli'. Nevertheless, I knew he'd have been disappointed to find out what sort of company I usually kept.

The Bedouin, of course, would claim they can run their own country any way they like, and that no jumped-up interlopers with PhDs have the right to barge in saying they know better because they're several generations away from tents.

There's an old chestnut of a joke in Jordan about the country's population. King Hussein visits China, where he mentions that his subjects total all of four million.

"Is that all?" says his Chinese host. "Why didn't you bring them with you to see the sights too?"

No, not very funny – but very true. As three-fifths of those four million are Palestinian, pure Jordanians are an endangered species. Another reason why they are nervous of the Palestinians, particularly when they hear calls for a Palestinian homeland that isn't necessarily made up of territory surrendered by Israel.

The arrests that had taken place the previous night at the concert had been of Palestinian youths. They'd been yelling slogans deemed offensive – anti-Israeli slogans were OK, but not slogans which criticised the rest of the Arab world for not helping the Palestinian cause. Some of the young men had been waving the PLO flag, flapping it in the giant face of King Hussein towering over the stage, and refusing to stop when ordered to do so.

"They've been given a home in Jordan," said Rathwan. "They are rude to wave their flag in front of our king's picture."

But I could understand the Palestinians' actions. The concert had got me so riled up myself, I was all set to storm the borders with a Kalishnikov; ill-mannered flag-waving seemed a fairly restrained response.

There are a lot of pictures of King Hussein in Jordan. There are a lot of pictures of Saddam Hussein in Iraq, but the difference is that the Jordanians put up pictures of their ruler voluntarily. He's ruled Jordan since he was eighteen, a country barely in existence then and firmly in the grip of British pashas. King Hussein rid himself of British advisers and anyone else who looked as if they'd try to manipulate him. Personally, at eighteen, if I'd been told I had to run a country, deal with the problem of Palestine and not necessarily have a soul near me I could trust, I'd have retired to my room in tears, probably with a lot of drugs.

I was fascinated by King Hussein. Jordan has borders with Syria, Saudi Arabia, Iraq and Israel; that Hussein had managed to keep his country from disappearing back into other people's sands was the basic testament to the man's intelligence. And he'd managed it without being a total brute to his subjects. Or anyone else's subjects: Syrians, Iraqis, Sudanese, Egyptians . . . anyone in the region who was in danger or couldn't earn enough to eat seemed to find their way to Jordan. It was telling that Amnesty International chose Amman for its regional base; and even the frustrated, put-upon Palestinians knew there was nowhere else in the Arab world that was as reasonable.

I also admired the way King Hussein succeeded in keeping the economy from Egyptian-style disaster – pretty fancy footwork given that Jordan has no oil and hardly a strip of arable land. All it has are tourists and a few blobs of potash.

And another thing about him: he doesn't look a fright, and that's always a bonus in a world leader. Even though he's old now, it's still plain to see that he never had to seek power in order to compensate for scaring himself when he looked in the mirror or not being able to pull the girls as a teenager – with quite a few rulers throughout history, you just know that's their problem.

When I first visited Petra, I was with my Australian army friend. As usual, she was keen on background information; supplying her with it was my job.

"So what's at Petra then?" she asked me.

I read aloud from my guidebook: "A city carved out of sandstone mountains, at least three thousand years old . . ." At the end, I added my own snippet of information: Petra was also famous as the scenery in the third Indiana Jones film, the one where Sean Connery played Harrison Ford's father and they . . .

My friend interrupted, excited: "Is that why they've got those

71

pictures of Sean Connery everywhere?" And she pointed to a picture of King Hussein.

Come to look at him, maybe when he was younger, at a glance . . . And when I heard he flew his own helicopter, and often turned up unheralded around town, screeching in unceremoniously on his motorbike . . . Well, that seemed like a pretty cool, James Bondy sort of king to me.

In England, in 1996, the Arms to Iraq scandal and the Scott Enquiry suggested a few things about cute King Hussein that didn't quite fit with my image of him as a Middle Eastern 007, fighting off all the bad guys for the little people. How did the Western world's arms get to Iraq so safely and unobtrusively despite the embargo against that country? Up the road past Abu Hamdi's castle.

Jordan, a country that had been known, if known at all, for the beauty of Petra and the glamour of the Bedouin, became the butt of satirical comedians' jokes, represented as a bear pit of dodgy arms dealers protected by Britain's dodgy civil servants. Ex-public school, Sandhurst-educated King Hussein might have had some very useful backhanders from fellow old boys in the Western arms trade to help claw his affable little country back from its constant verge of bankruptcy. And there might have been the odd used fiver from Saddam Hussein as well, as payment for such a reliable delivery service in his time of need.

So, very like England, Jordan runs a society of easygoing, reasonably well-fed tolerance on some extremely nasty fuel. Except it's easier for a terrified, starving refugee to get into Jordan. Perhaps because any income, dodgy or otherwise, goes towards enriching the country, not lining King Hussein's own pockets. He has a vision, not just personal greed and ambition.

As the historical home of the Arab Revolt, Jordan is something of a 'promised land' to the king. He's taken the stigma of Jordan being an artificially created state, a strip of fenced-off sand, and tried to turn it around; he's made a country which, should it be un-invented, would be sorely missed by anyone looking for an oasis in the region.

Nevertheless, dear old James Bond would have turned in his licence if he'd noticed what important international chaps were really like. Long before he was twenty, King Hussein must have realised that just being a handsome nice chap would have been worse than useless to his precariously placed people in a world of very bad eggs.

The men who'd tormented me when I'd parked the car were grouped around it the following morning. Had they been waiting all night to help me steer out? I felt a little churlish when I realised that they were there to show me that the front tyre was completely flat. Rathwan's generous friend would probably break his other arm over my head – hadn't he told us not to drive in the desert? Hadn't we blithely trundled over rocky gravel to Abu Hamdi's house, bounced up dirt tracks to desert castles? Blaming Rathwan for everything, I found the spare tyre in the boot – another flat. Much arm-waving and shouting from the onlookers.

"Don't worry," said Rathwan. "Wait here."

He went off with two of the men in a battered brown Mercedes. The remaining spectators nodded at me sympathetically.

"You hire this car, lady?" one of them asked.

"It belongs to a friend."

He passed this around the crowd for discussion. To console me, one of the men gave me a sticky cake from a box he was carrying. After a worryingly long time, Rathwan reappeared with a tyre. Every man present involved himself in fitting it – except Rathwan, who lolled in the doorway of one of the shoe shops debating the crisis with an old man who'd arrived too late to get a hand to the wheel. As for me, it was all well and good to get on my high driving seat about men assuming I couldn't park – but I had to stand by admitting to myself that I'd never changed a tyre. When the job was done everyone was euphoric, as if we'd got a kitten down from a tree or a child out of a well. I didn't clench one irritated tooth as a million hands directed me out of the parking space in a thousand contradictory ways.

"Did it cost much for a new tyre?" I asked Rathwan.

"It's not new but it's better than the one before. Really, I tell you Annie, this man is not my friend, he's a bastard. We could have had a terrible accident."

"He did tell us to keep to the road."

"No. He is a bastard. He knows I'll give him some money for lending the car but he doesn't say the car is dangerous. I'll give him nothing. Really, believe me, he's a bastard. Maybe we'll keep the car, he's such a bastard."

He calmed down gradually and was hardly saying 'bastard' at all by the time we reached the sleepy little town of Ajlun.

"Ajlun is nice, the people here are very gentle, not like Amman."

I said nothing, hoping for the gentle people's sake that none of them did anything to stir Rathwan up again.

Challenging the country for miles around, Ar-Rabad castle stands high above Ajlun. On the way up to it, we had lunch at the Al-Rabad Hotel – a meal that made us both feel no one would ever be a bastard again. White linen tablecloths on a vine-shaded terrace; the castle above, green-splashed russet fields and the dusty yellow of the town below. I suspect whoever translated the menu sat on the terrace to work and was distracted by the sheer blaze of the view; or they were drunk, or they were poring industriously over a dictionary compiled by a drunk. Customers could choose from: 'succulent tropical tuna with thing'; 'pearl wheat mixed with finely chopped tomato and capricious parsley'; 'chicken with a bevy of tomato'; 'tow fresh eggs whicked'; 'Egyptian red bean stew with fresh tomato or smack of garlic'; 'slices of meat with oriental'; or 'rice mixed with tomato, parsley, olive oil rolled in graves leaves and cooked over a light byre cornered with lemon juice'.

We read out the menu to each other, choking back laughter in front of the sweet-natured waiter in case the verbal tossed salad was his hard work. After tomato bevys and graves leaves we lounged with coffee and chocolate ice cream ('ice cream chocolate struck with wafer') watching the stretch of land ahead, undisturbed by other customers or any formed thoughts. A kestrel soared across the sky.

Rathwan said, "That's how my heart feels when I look at you."

Qala'at ar-Rabad was once part of a chain of beacons and pigeon posts for sending news from Syria to Cairo. It's claimed that on a clear day you can see Jerusalem from the castle. We didn't, but the almost-forever spread of land in every direction was exciting enough. But sitting soaking it all in was a little spoilt by a hideously loud generator behind the ticket booth. Rathwan declared the generator a bastard but didn't go on about it; instead, he leant against a rock reading his newspaper while I, being foreign, climbed all over the ruins for half an hour.

The castle was built in the twelfth century as a defence against the Crusaders by Saladin's brother. Saladin: now there was a man among . . . well, men probably. Mohammed's favourite wife, Ayesha, led her own army, but after the death of the Prophet, Islam hadn't done more than any other religion to get women up and at it. How had women's career prospects looked in Saladin's time? How, for that matter, did they look now? I knew as little about the women of Jordan as I knew about Saladin – but I could look him up in a book. Salah ad-Din was a Kurd who'd led the Arab armies, driven out the Crusaders and established the Ayyubid dynasty that ruled Egypt, Syria and Western Arabia for almost a hundred years. There wasn't enough on him in my guidebook to make me a Saladin expert, but I was a lot better off than I had been. As I told Rathwan, I was sure I remembered being given the impression in school lessons that Saladin had lost the Crusades.

"Of course he won." Rathwan looked at me aghast. Oh yes, he was quite the know-all on history and ancient monuments but he'd just make vague remarks, like "It depends on the family" or "Their freedom increases all the time", when I asked him about the lives of present-day Jordanian women.

We pottered around Ajlun town for a while to put off the evil hour when we'd have to return the car. There seemed to be a plethora of small shops selling huge pink dresses.

"Wedding dresses," Rathwan said. "Would you like one of them?"

Imagining myself lumbering around in one of these explosions of lace and frothed taffeta flounces, I said I thought not.

He looked at me thoughtfully.

"I think you would prefer to get married in trousers. Isn't this an expression in English, the wife wears the trousers?"

I tried to disentangle him from his confusion, but we ended up with far too many trousers – a wife in metaphorical trousers, her husband still in actual trousers, and the wife possibly also in real trousers but not necessarily . . .

Back in Amman, I had a sinking feeling as we drew up to the car-owner's house.

"There's not going to be a big argument is there?" I tried to introduce a pink-wedding-dress edge of frail femininity into my voice. I didn't know Rathwan well enough to be sure how he might be in an argument. Would I be taking him back to the Hotel Wadi with a broken nose, or looking for the car-owner's relatives to get them to tend *his* broken nose?

"No, no," Rathwan soothed me. "Of course not. I will explain what happened clearly and calmly. Don't worry, I will wear our trousers for this."

The owner clucked around his car. Suspiciously soon, he noticed one of the tyres was different and immediately accused me of driving in the desert. I avoided actually denying the charge.

"The tyre was worn. They're all worn."

The man gave me a disappointed look, then said something nasty in Arabic. Rathwan's eyes flickered dangerously but he kept very calm. He talked a great deal, quietly, relentlessly. The owner pitched from arrogance to extreme nervousness, and hurriedly took the keys from me.

"Yes. Thank you. Goodbye."

"What did you say to him?"

"He said the tyre was our fault and you should pay him something. I told him he was lucky we didn't have an accident that killed you. He would have had to pay thousands of dinar to your parents or go to prison."

"I don't think that's how it would work."

"He doesn't know this."

It didn't seem fair. The man had lent us the car and we had driven it in the desert; he was only little and he had a broken arm . . .

"No, Annie, don't be sorry. Believe me, there is more to this story. You know really why he lent his car? He is Egyptian. He has no work permit. He knows I have relatives in the ministry and can help him. But yesterday he gets a work permit without me, so lending his car is wasted. So he's using any excuse to get money. You see the kind of bastard?"

I was sick of the whole thing, and particularly sick of the word 'bastard'.

"I wish we'd never borrowed the car if you're going to be like this."

He looked at me astonished. "I'm not 'like this'. But really this man is a bastard."

He installed me at the terrace cafe opposite the Roman theatre with tea and a copy of the *Star*, a local English-language paper, before heading off in search of Bashir and Salah.

"We will have fun with them. You'll be happy again."

I'd been unable to shake off my guilt about the car man. I worried about what had really been said in Arabic; the man had seemed quite frightened at the end. I worried about how little I knew Rathwan.

But when he'd been gone five minutes, I cheered up. I abandoned my newspaper, preferring to watch the people wandering through the gardens below, a pageant of variations on the theme of Arab dress. Two children were trying to catch the little stray cats scooting in and out of the bushes or shading themselves under benches. The tiny animals had the elegant faces of cat statues in ancient Egyptian tombs. They were all over the gardens and the amphitheatre, always looking surprisingly clean; a fallen nobility, used to better things than the underside of a park bench but keeping up their standards all the same. One of the children made a grab for a cat, the cat scratched and the game was over.

As I watched the consoling mother shake her fists at all cats, I felt eyes boring into the back of my head. I turned to meet a fixed contemptuous glare from a group of men at the table behind me. They were wearing white robes, white *kefiyah* and gold watches. I was wearing a dark cotton shirt that came to my wrists and loose trousers that came to my ankles. I wasn't showing anything that I shouldn't be, was doing them no harm at all – but they muttered to each other, making no attempt to hide their sneering discussion of me. They were unashamedly hostile. It's very hard to pick up your newspaper and ignore all that spite in the corner of your eye, but when I glared back at them, the muttering grew worse. If I'd been sitting there pulling pages out of the Koran and hurling them over the balcony for the cats to play with, I might have been doing something to deserve the way they were talking about me.

The men smirked nastily as they saw two policemen approach my table. I smirked back as I shook hands with Bashir and Salah, and tried to look as though I was lodging a complaint. Rathwan, coming smiling along behind his friends, was cleared of all doubt, I was so relieved to see him.

I didn't tell tales on my charming neighbours until they'd left the cafe, afraid Rathwan would do something drastic if they were still in clouting distance.

"Oh, they are probably from the Gulf or Saudi Arabia. They're not used to foreign women."

"That's no excuse for being so horrible."

"They probably weren't being horrible deliberately. It's just curiosity."

If that was curiosity no wonder it was the one thing that could kill a cat.

Over dinner, the conversation turned to weddings. Bashir was getting married soon and moaning about it.

"You see, Annie, in Jordan it's very expensive to get married. For instance, there is the gold. You have seen the gold market on King Faisal Street?"

I had: shop after shop with windows curtained in gold chains, 'Midas Was Here' mounds of rings, bracelets piled on trays . . .

"The man must give gold to his wife. Me, for instance, an ordinary policeman, I must give at least one thousand dinar worth of gold to her. And new dresses and the wedding dress. Also new dresses for her sisters and her mother and father. I have to give a television to her father. Then there is a feast to buy, a big feast. I even have to pay the cost of the cars to and back from the feast."

Poor Bashir had already shelled out well over three thousand dinar, and his fiancée was complaining that he was mean.

"I must think of the future. A house, mattresses and pots in the house. She only sees today."

"But you like her."

"Oh yes, I love her," Bashir glowed. "She is very beautiful. Blonde like you. But not brave like you, travelling everywhere. She likes to stay at home because she is afraid even from a very small butterfly, from a dog, a cat, a chicken or a small cock."

Rathwan gave me a warning look. Bashir showed me a picture of his timid flower: a welterweight of a girl in a shoulder-padded, electric-blue suit, harshly dyed blonde hair and a look in her eye that would scare off any small cocks at fifty paces.

Bashir patted the photograph gently. "She is very sweet, Annie, you will like her."

I hoped to God she'd like me, or I wouldn't last to the first bell.

The talk shifted into Arabic. Rathwan was funny enough in

English but he obviously brought the house down in his own language. Bashir and Salah were almost face down in their dinners, they were so convulsed with laughter.

"I'm telling them about our visit to Abu Hamdi," Rathwan explained.

I didn't think we'd been with Abu Hamdi as long as it took Rathwan to tell what had happened. I decided he must be making things up.

When he'd eventually had his last laugh, it was Salah's turn to tell a story. His eyes sparkled, his voice switched through what seemed to be a series of impersonations, his hands flew in and out of gestures. The listening was as intense as his effort in the telling, Rathwan and Bashir never taking their eyes off him. The complex yarn came to rest after a good ten minutes. Rathwan and Bashir sighed and nodded appreciatively. A good story.

"Sorry," Rathwan apologised to me. "Salah was telling us that a relative of his was arrested for being drunk and was brought to Salah's station. Salah intervened, telling the others not to lock the man up because he was normally a very good man, and so he got him released."

"That was it?"

"Yes."

"But it was a very long story when Salah told it."

Bashir laughed. "English speaking like this . . ." – indicating a straight line with one hand – "Arabs speaking like this . . ." – weaving both hands elaborately in and out.

We took the elaborate talk to the Roman theatre. Ismat seemed pleased to be visited, but glanced past us warily before locking the gates, just in case there were any nocturnal boys around.

We'd bought him a watermelon from one of the hut-size mounds of them sold by the roadside in summer. Ismat hacked up the fruit with a penknife and made tea on his kerosene stove. The Roman theatre was a magic place at night, gently floodlit, with the gates locked against the rest of the city, only the special friends of Ismat allowed in. It felt vaguely naughty to be there, as if we were children who'd broken into a deserted mansion to play house.

The topic of Bashir's wedding returned. The expense of a bride was bemoaned. I asked how anyone who wasn't a millionaire could afford more than one wife, let alone the legally permitted four.

"This is why young men now have usually just one wife – the expense," Rathwan said. "In the desert it is different. They pay each other in sheep and goats, they can have four wives. But for someone like Bashir, it is all money."

Ismat had four wives in his time, but only one was alive now. In his day it was easier, the bride price situation hadn't got out of hand: a few jewels, a moderate feast. But of course, he added with a smile, all this was a thousand years ago.

It seemed hardly encouraging to the growth of Bedouin numbers if would-be husbands and fathers were being priced out of the market. The system gave a value to female children – unlike some cultures where a woman had to bring a dowry with her to get a husband; cultures where girl babies were aborted, abandoned, had their skulls crushed with stones . . . Any desperate measure in poor families to avoid the expense of a daughter.

Yet a wife who'd essentially been bought didn't seem to me to be starting married life on a very equal footing.

Bashir said the gold a man had to pay was usually not a problem in the long run; it was an investment that could be returned to him to sell if the family ran short of money. But there could be a snag. Sometimes the wife could refuse – he clutched his hands to his chest, pouting and putting on a squeaky voice – "No, it's for me!"

Ismat suspected that about ten years ago there was a big secret meeting in the desert between all the women, and all the men who sell gold: "And they decide to work together in this."

We sat around the closed-down ruins on old oil cans and cushions, eating watermelon chunks and drinking tea. A few other policemen arrived. There was kissing and hugging and laddish arm-thumping, more long stories and gales of laughter – as if it was everyone's birthday and several vats of alcohol had been consumed instead of Ismat's sweet, sage-flavoured tea. If it weren't for social respectability and the dwindling Bedouin population, who needed wives? There was all this inexpensive fun to be had with the boys.

CHAPTER 4

On the Women's Side of the Tent

It was hot enough to induce hysteria at the slightest inconvenience. As the streets were so crowded, there was considerable inconvenient bumping and shoving. I could feel myself getting into the pleasant frame of mind of Robert De Niro in *Taxi Driver*. Amman was never quiet but it was usually a city of courteous amblers and street-corner idlers; crowds drifted lightly past each other, as mellow as the air that always seemed softly scented with caramel. Now someone had put amphetamines in the water and spoilt everything. People sped and barged and cursed – even the sweet air smelt goaty, petrolly, armpitty and anything else that was sharp and assaulting. There was a panic on – the last shopping day before Eid al Adhah, the Feast of the Sacrifice. Businesses would close for up to a week, families would visit each other bearing gifts, but first there was the riot and pillage of last-chance preparation.

It's estimated that over three hundred and fifty thousand sheep and goats are sacrificed in the Muslim world on this feast day. Eid al Adhah commemorates God sparing Abraham the sacrifice of his son Isaac; it also marks the end of the Haj, the main pilgrimage to Mecca. I watched extraordinary scenes of the pilgrims on television; it looked as if all the people in the world were dressed in white, moving across the desert with determined devotion. I remembered once, in my long-lapsed Catholic past, attending a papal audience – compared to these scenes it had all the spirituality of the football terraces, with the pope's arrival provoking a reaction like a goal scored. Then the pope called out the names of groups attending, like a compere at a supporters' club dinner: "Is there anyone in from Poland tonight? God bless you Poland and thank you for coming. Hope you'll enjoy the mass we've got lined up for you, some very talented altar boys are coming up later and there'll be an all-star benediction at nine o'clock." We were herded in, herded out – I didn't feel a thing. Yet even through the television, I could feel the deep cuts Islam made in the consciousness of the believer: belief lived every hour, forming an identical pattern beneath a thousand different ways of life.

Of course, all the people in the world weren't at Mecca because there were an awful lot of them left to push me around Amman – buying, buying, buying. The shop windows were stacked with bright-ribboned displays of cakes, biscuits and sweets, being boxed and bought as urgently as they were replaced by perspiring bakers and confectioners. Monkey-heaven loads of nuts were scooped into plastic bags, and dead chickens on strings were whacked out at customers by manic poulterers. Fruit and vegetables were tumbling from stalls to make ankle-deep squelch piles as they were too-hastily sold by demented, hands-flying vendors; old Bedouin men teetered away carrying crates of oranges, hedges of coriander, towns of tomatoes and sacks of potatoes the size of airships. Women clawed dresses from the racks in clothes shops, flapped new head scarves for their daughters to try on, pushed little sons' feet into stiff new shoes, snapping at any child who wasn't fully co-operating with the drive to get the family up to scratch in time. Money was being spent and needed replacing, so the queues at the banks were endless.

Rathwan had to join one of the queues and warned me he might be gone for some time. Despite the clamour at the count-ers, the bank felt like a soothing chapel of meditation compared to the scenes outside; it was crisply modern, efficient and air-conditioned. I leant against the wall and slipped my shoes off to feel the cool marble floors, perfectly happy to be out of the fraught streets for as long as it took. The respite from fighting to move an inch ahead along the pavements came just in time to stop me screaming abuse at Rathwan, blaming him for the crowd, the hole in the ozone layer and anything else that occurred to me.

Into the late-twentieth-century world of commerce and com-puters stepped a tiny woman straight out of a back issue of *National Geographic*, a perfect traditional Bedouin. Her leathery face and hands were covered in blue tribal tattoos. She had heavy gold earrings and bracelets, and gold rings on her tattooed fingers. Her floral-patterned head scarf was tied up in a way that made her head look pointy. (I don't know if the pointy-head look serves any purpose, but Rathwan has a theory that it makes these usually small women look taller.) A thin black veil flowed down her back to cover her hair; her black dress, with bright embroidery at the shoulders, reached to her tiny feet.

There was something about the style of these desert women that leaned more to the Romany than the imprisoning sobriety usually associated with Islamic female dress. The desert women were modestly well covered, but personality and vigour flashed through in touches of colour and unmasked faces. I had seen diluted versions of this woman around town but this was like looking at a souvenir doll, her appearance was so uncompromising – except that they probably wouldn't have made a souvenir doll carrying a bright red plastic dustpan and broom. The nylon bristles on the broom were wrapped in polythene so I guessed that she'd just bought this incongruous item. Even more incongruously, she was with a tall, beautiful Arab girl in chic Western clothes; the girl's long, wavy hair was uncovered, her skirt was a little too far above the knee for Jordan, her heels too high for comfort on Amman's potholed pavements.

The unlikely pair were standing in the doorway discussing something, when they caught sight of me and stopped mid-sentence. The young woman looked away when she met my eyes; the older one stared on unabashed, then smiled at me revealing a mouth well graced with gold teeth. They hurriedly exchanged a few more words, then retreated to the street.

Rathwan was beside me, flustered. "I've just seen my aunt. Wait here for me."

He dashed into the street but returned a few minutes later looking disappointed.

"She is my favourite aunt and I've missed her. Did you see her?"

"What does she look like?"

"A small Bedouin woman with a young daughter." Of course.

The vision from *National Geographic* was Auntie, with a daughter who'd clearly fallen very far from the tree. I looked at Rathwan in his denim shirt and jeans, holding a bank book, his Walkman in his top pocket.

"Sometimes I can't believe it," I said.

"Believe what?"

"How you're in two places at once."

He looked at me as if I'd grown heads in two places at once and went back to his place in the queue.

The Hotel Wadi staff came jumping and shouting into the street, helping with our luggage and waving us off. They seemed to be more excited about our going away for the holiday than we were ourselves. The morning we'd spent on Amman's frantic pre-holiday streets had trampled most of our potential for jumping and shouting.

We finally transferred from our traffic-snarled city taxi to a long-distance service taxi – a Peugeot with an overload of big, hairy, cross-looking men holding dainty boxes of cakes in big, hairy hands. Just when I was sure one more mile in the Peugeot would suffocate me, we escaped, falling out of the car doors in Mafraq, a town on the northern edge of the desert; everyone here was rushing about with cake boxes or rushing to buy some. Rathwan talked a passer-by into giving us a lift to a Bedouin village further out in the desert.

"Do you know this man?" I asked, as we bumped along in his four-wheel-drive Toyota.

"No, but I recognise him. He sometimes works in our village. He mends wooden things."

We headed south-east for about an hour, Rathwan and the wooden-thing mender chatting and laughing like long-lost brothers. Out in the Eastern Desert, life was still lived by very old rules. If you could, you helped anyone who asked for assistance – unless they were notorious for axe-murdering – because the next day you might need their help to survive. This Bedouin tradition had become a pillar of Islam; beggars must always be given alms, just as a destitute stranger arriving at your tent had to be given food and water. Rathwan wasn't quite the miraculous charmer of his fellow citizens he often appeared to be; he merely played expertly on the spirit of charity inherent in his culture.

In the city and in more tourist-worn areas, the notion of selfishness as a better survival technique had begun to take some hold. The Bedouin down in Wadi Rum charged people to stay in their tents and Petra was awash with a competitive greed that Rathwan found very distasteful. He had to go to those popular tourist areas for his work but he was happiest in the Eastern Desert where he didn't meet so many Bedouin who were a disappointment to him. Resentment, loss of self-respect and genuine destitution scabbed the surface of lives where the old values had been abandoned. In part, this had come about because tourists had exploited the openness of traditional Bedouin society; no need to bring much spending money when a meal and shelter could be cadged off the friendly locals. I wondered if the generosity of the entire country, with its borders open to the refugees of the Muslim world, would eventually be exploited to the point where it would turn bitter and shrivel in on its own interests. But, for the time being, out in the desert it was still very bad form to say 'No' when you could possibly say 'Yes'.

The Bedouin village we eventually arrived at was typical of its kind: a sprawling collection of breeze-block houses centred around a school, a small mosque and an all-purpose shop. Goats, sheep and chickens strolled the stony lanes between houses and washing lines bunted between electricity poles. Many of the houses were only half-finished, with metal rods sticking up out of flat roofs – further storeys could be added as the family's wealth increased or its numbers multiplied.

Sometimes, a harsh winter would drive Bedouin from their tents to villages like this. More often, village living was to accommodate the children's compulsory schooling or to provide a gentler home for the sick and the old. There were a number of true desert-dwelling men, like Rathwan's father with his two wives and seventeen children, who split their households between tent and village, leaving the lesser-favoured wife in the village to look after the children at school.

As Bedouin made up such a large percentage of King Hussein's police force and armed services, many of the younger generation needed village homes for easier access to their work. Bedouin loyalty to him was one of the few things King Hussein could trust as he kept up his walk-on-water act through the storms of Middle Eastern politics. The Bedouin villages were heavily subsidised by the government and hundreds of miles of government land was kept available for the nomadic Bedouin to manoeuvre in. They protected him; he indulged them.

I stood surrounded by luggage and curious children while Rathwan went off in search of our next lift. It was getting dark and I wondered where on earth I was. Somewhere way past the last town marked on the map, in the blank space before you hit the Iraqi border. To pass the time I tried out some Arabic, asking the children their names. This seemed to scare them. They ran shrieking for cover behind a battered Mercedes; even their dog followed them. Safely barricaded from the scary woman, they popped their heads up and kept shouting, in English, "What is your name? What is your name?"

I told them, several times, but this obviously wasn't a good enough answer. I saw a policeman from the Desert Patrol come hurrying towards me and wondered if I'd committed some unwitting act of child molestation. But then I realised he was with Rathwan.

"This is my friend. He'll take us to my father's tent."

The Desert Patrol dress was a glamorous mix of traditional Bedouin and modern military attire. They had red-and-white *kefiyah* with a silver badge of office on the front, and long khaki tunics crossed with leather bandoliers and heavy gunbelts; sometimes a khaki shirt and trousers replaced the tunic.

The men of the Desert Patrol were something of a tourist attraction, but they had a proper job to do alongside looking decorative on postcards. Tourists got lost in the desert, headed dangerously close to unfriendly borders or tried to disport themselves on military firing ranges, and needed re-channelling to more suitable routes. Then there were occasional territorial disputes between Bedouin and private landowners over sheep mashing through watermelons, goats gorging through herb gardens, tents on a tract newly acquired for private enterprise – new world and old driving each other crazy.

The Desert Patrol would sometimes be asked to intervene in disputes among the Bedouin themselves, although many of these internal problems were still judged and sorted by tribal elders in protracted negotiations over coffee."I am in your face," you'd say, as you flung yourself on the mercy of your tribal elder once you'd committed your crime, and he would give you sanctuary while he investigated the matter. Perhaps the offended party would agree to a settlement; perhaps they'd want you prosecuted. Or dead – in which case, it was best to scarper for a few years and eventually start long-distance negotiations once tempers had cooled. Although settlements out of the legal mainstream were more usual, the tribal elders had to call in the Desert Patrol if the situation got too colourful; Rathwan would often read me tales from the local papers of Wild West-style shoot-outs over sheep rustling that required a Desert Patrol posse to simmer them down. Insult-avenging was still known to escalate into a blood bath and, occasionally, like the rest of us, the Bedouin just murdered each other. Stabbed husbands formed an interestingly high crime statistic. Exciting stuff for the Desert Patrol if they were called in, but they spent most of their time guarding vital installations out in the far sands – radio masts, pumping stations and their dull like.

Our personal representative from the Desert Patrol had a sturdy four-wheel drive and we set out across the dark, rocky sands.

"How do we know where we're going?"

"We're Bedouin, we can follow the stars."

"Really?"

"No. But I asked in the village. My father's tents are about a mile to the east – and the jeep has a compass."

Rathwan translated this exchange for the patrolman, who laughed, then made a serious comment.

"He says old Bedouin know the stars but it is dying out now. He says his father knows the stars. Mine does too. We are both very bad sons."

Rathwan didn't seem all that ashamed of his filial shortcomings: he was more interested in learning how the CB radio worked.

After an hour of bucketing around, hitting rocks and doing a lot more of what looked like guesswork rather than any sort of trained desert orienteering, we found Rathwan's family. I saw an odd, yet strangely familiar light coming out of the darkness ahead of us. As we got closer I realised what it was: the flickering glow of a television set. Plugged into the battery of a four-wheel drive, the television eerily illuminated the open-fronted section of a large goatskin tent, with the family watching intently as they stretched out on mattresses around the embers of a fire.

When we drew up, children, small goats and chickens skittered about – the animals fleeing from the sudden disruption, the children coming to see what had arrived. Rathwan's father stood, switched off the television and waited for us to come to him. A rapid disappearance was made by two women I'd glimpsed when we got out of the jeep.

The patrolman politely declined an offer of tea and drove off with all the confidence of a man who'd forgotten he didn't know how to find his way all that well by any means. One of the women then came back into the open area of the tent: this was Farriad, the father's young, pretty third wife. She was known as Umm Tahir: mother of Tahir, her eldest son. Men would be known as Abu . . . – father of . . . – after their eldest son. (Eldest daughters didn't get to rename their parents.)

Umm Tahir was laughing as she greeted us and talking to someone behind the heavy cloth that partitioned off another section of the tent. I heard a young woman's voice; she sounded as though she was complaining about something.

Rathwan talked to the mystery voice, then told me, "It is my sister Alia. She won't come out. She thinks you are a man with your short hair and trousers."

In traditional households, the womenfolk have to remain out of view if a male visitor arrives who isn't a close family friend or a relative. If the visitor is something that looks like neither fish nor fowl, good girls like Alia play it safe and retreat anyway.

Alia did eventually emerge. Still wary, she looked me up and down; then, just about convinced of my gender, she shook hands. She had a nice face: plump and pretty, with pale olive skin. She wore a white head scarf and a plain black overdress, with so many other layers beneath it that it was hard to tell what was her and what was dresses.

Rathwan looked like his father: the same handsome features and stocky build, but at around five foot ten, quite tall for Jordanians; they had the same charismatic, ebullient air and the same eyes. Perhaps because he kept his head covered with a *kefiyah*, Father's fifty-year-old face looked less weather-beaten and was paler than Rathwan's. He was expansively welcoming, offering us tea and sharing out the cakes we'd brought – excited at the distraction but not quite to the somersault-turning extent of some of his younger sons.

Umm Tahir was twenty-seven, had five children and another one on the way. So, if there were three from Rathwan's mother, the second wife must have had nine children to make up the full set of seventeen Rathwan had quoted me. He had to think hard to even remember the names of all his brothers and sisters; luckily for my name-remembering capacity, they weren't all at the tent. There was just Alia, Umm Tahir's five, and three of the second wife's children.

Rathwan had a close, teasing rapport with Alia; his other full sister was married and lived elsewhere. He admitted that his sisters were the ones he really cared about; he just felt a vague fondness for the others, with one or two particular favourites emerging from the herd. There was Khalid, a twenty-two-year-old who was away in the army; Rathwan felt close to him as he was the nearest male in age – he looked out for Khalid and advised him. Of the children currently at the tent, it was Yousef he liked the most, simply because he was such a likeable child. One of the second wife's sons, Yousef was small for his eight years, full of beans, with funny, sticking-out hair and a big smile. He chatted to me enthusiastically, throwing all the English he'd learnt in school at me in long barmy sentences, shrieking with delight if I managed a long barmy Arabic sentence back. He showed me what he called 'a small sheep' – a lamb – which had a bad leg and was his special charge. "No leg here, see. Leg in one month."

In strict Bedouin society, it is bad manners to ask a stranger a lot of questions; the visitor should offer information first. Rathwan talked at length to his father, who kept looking at me and nodding. Rathwan was offering information on my behalf: where I was from, what I was doing and so on. At the end of my potted life history, his father simply said that I was very welcome.

Many glasses of strong, sweet tea later, the family spread around the tent for the night. Two-section tents were more common, but this had four large sections – Rathwan's father was a wealthy man. Rathwan, a sixteen-year-old brother and their father slept in the *shiig*, the open-fronted, public section of the tent. Alia led me behind the mystery curtain to *al muhram*, more commonly transcribed in English as 'the harem' – it just means the women's part of the tent, nothing kinky. Beyond that was a section where Umm Tahir slept with her two youngest children, then another large section where cooking and housekeeping (tentkeeping) chores were done. In our section, we lay down on a row of foam mattresses, Alia at one end, me at the other, with the little boys between us. We had cosy duvets – the same cotton duvet covers as I used at home but stuffed with sheep's wool. I noticed Alia slept with all her clothes on, so I kept all mine on

97

too and hoped I wouldn't have to go to the toilet in the night.

Rathwan had talked me through this one: just go out into the desert to the west of the tent, he'd said. Making the trip with a torch earlier on hadn't been too hair-raising, but the idea of stumbling around out there in the black nothingness while everyone else was asleep . . . Or worse, stumbling around and mortifyingly waking up the whole household and half the goats . . . Not only was I worried that all the tea I'd drunk hadn't got through my system, I had the irritation of a period to contend with as well in these intrepid-explorer surroundings. Didn't happen to Wilfred Thesiger, that was for sure. I wondered what Gertrude Bell had done?

I lay awake for a while, listening to the funny squeaking sound children make when they're asleep, and the occasional flap of the tent in the light breeze. The small sheep bleated somewhere nearby; its no leg must have been playing up. Or perhaps it could see into the tent and was troubled by an unexpected sight – a row of little dark heads and then a big blonde one. The little dark head next to me, Yousef, seemed to be having a nightmare; he made a sudden yelping sound and grabbed frantically at the air above him. I took his hands and held them; they relaxed and I tucked them back under his covers. He turned towards me, opened his eyes momentarily and instead of screaming with fright at having his nightmare turn to reality – yes, there *was* a large, strange-looking thing in the room – he smiled and settled down again. Then the whole row of heads slept.

It was before five when I heard Rathwan's father come quietly into our section. He woke Yousef by gently pulling at his ears and whispering to him; after a few seconds of confusion, Yousef rubbed his eyes and staggered out after his father. Ten minutes later, Alia was rustling her skirts; she crept off towards the cooking part of the tent. The sun was up, so Bedouin were up. Not wanting a reputation as a lazy, no-good foreigner I forced myself out of my cosy nest into the sharp morning air. I remembered that before I took on the world of tent-dwelling with any enthusiasm, I had to deal with my bathroom situation.

I know T.E. Lawrence didn't fill the *Seven Pillars of Wisdom* with a great many accounts of where he went to the toilet – actually, in the case of the glamorous Lawrence of Arabia I'd prefer not to believe he went to the toilet at all – but as a more humble mortal I have a mind forced along these vulgar channels by a domineering, undisciplined body.

The change in food or climate had unexpectedly brought on my period. Not only being an unglamorous traveller but also a disorganised one, I hadn't brought anything as sensible as tampons with me. My punishment for having a scrambled sort of mind was a harrowing experience in Downtown Amman trying to buy what I needed.

I looked in my phrasebook for any word approximating what I wanted. Not a thing. I had to broach the matter with Rathwan; I could see he was having to make considerable allowances and feeling that he was being extremely broadminded to be involved in a discussion of the subject at all. (Although he later referred to it as my 'human problem', which is far nicer than any Western euphemism.) He knew no useful Arabic to help solve my

99

predicament. Then he said he would do anything for me, I must be sure of that, but he could not, even at gunpoint, go into a shop and ask for such things.

We decided that it was probably best to head for a pharmacy; I imagined I'd find one with a kindly matron behind the counter who would help me. I skipped the first shop we passed, run by intimidating, white-coated young men. The second pharmacy was also staffed by men. Rathwan now told me that he didn't think many women worked in these shops; maybe I should go in anyway, perhaps I would just see what I wanted and pick it up or point to it.

Eyes scanning around as I went in, I braved the second shop. It was like a little pharmacy of yesteryear: all the wares in glass cases and a single central counter offering delightful, old-fashioned, personal service – no alienating aisles of goods where I could just grab the needful and make a swift exit without discussion. All I could see on the shelves were medicines, ointments and forty shades of toothbrush. Thinking the brand name would be universal, I asked for Tampax. The man behind the counter looked at me as if I'd walked in topless, and sharply said, "No!" Rathwan and I found another shop, where my request for Tampax was greeted with the same affronted look and definite "NO." It occurred to me the word Tampax might sound dangerously like Durex; perhaps I should stand in the middle of the next shop reciting all the other possible brand names at the top of my voice.

Following me from shop to shop but remaining outside at a safe distance with the phrasebook, Rathwan had come up with the Arabic for 'tissues'. He taught me to say 'women's tissues', and I headed into yet another pharmacy to give it a try, hoping I wouldn't be beaten from the doors as a cannibal. The young man behind this counter had a pleasant smile. He was serving a pair of old men with bottles of pills but interrupted his transaction to ask what I would like. I pretended not to understand and looked around the shelves; I felt I could share my problem with the young man but the old ones were off-putting. They were examining the pills closely, as if they were in a contest to guess how many there were in the bottles. Finally, convinced that they had enough pills for their money, they left.

As I'd seen nothing approximating 'women's tissues' on the shelves, I tried my peculiar turn of phrase on the young man. He stared at me, completely baffled, then grinned and said in English, "Wrong shop."

He led me to a shop two doors away that seemed to sell nuts and dried beans – 'women's tissues' had obviously mistranslated very badly. The young man spoke in rapid Arabic. The dried bean man gave me a look of contempt and reached under the counter to produce a box of those massive sanitary towels with loops. There was a picture of a very lusty-looking Western woman on the box and the product was called New Cinderella.

In case you're asking, because I did, desert women simply wash their periods away or use scrap pieces of cloth that they burn afterwards. If you're wearing a big dress and living a segregated life, you don't have to spend a fortune every month keeping your secret.

New Cinderella were not exactly handy for travel. Luckily

my tent garb was a shirt that reached almost to the knees of my jeans, so any embarrassing bulges were hidden. But where could I hide myself? From the tent's position, on top of a small hill, I could see for miles across stony wastes. A landscape where an over-large ant's movements would be clearly visible. No trees, just a few thistles; plenty of rocks, not one of them bigger than me. I walked for ages, hoping somehow to get out of sight of the tent, wishing I had a big Bedouin dress I could just squat down in. Then I found heaven: a small cave going down into the ground. I scrambled into it, glad it didn't stretch back too far where lions and tigers and bears might be lurking. It was just big enough to stand up in and there was even a piece of wood that I could use to bury my unpleasant leavings. I knew I was being ecologically unsound – I should have burnt my New Cinderella before burial – but having found a private space I didn't want to draw attention to it by sending up smoke signals. I thanked the desert for making the cave for me; I thanked the Western world for inventing Wet Wipes – something I did have the common sense to bring with me. I felt refreshed, felt I wouldn't be put out of the tent for smelling, and went back to see how the day was shaping up.

Alia handed me a jug of water. "For washing the hands and face, Yan," she said in English. ('Yan' was her version of my name.) I used Alia's water for my face and hands but wimpishly cleaned my teeth with mineral water; to be taken sick out here trying to be intrepid would be the humiliating end of the world.

Alia returned to making bread, the first of her usual daily tasks. The flour-and-water dough was left in a basin overnight after an hour's strenuous kneading; come morning, it was cooked over a wood fire, on what looked like a large, upturned wok. Small blobs of dough were pulled into flattish rounds, then slung on the wok. The cooking was deft: the dough baked quickly on the scalding surface and had to be turned over within seconds; at the turn it also had to be stretched to get the bread as thin as paper. Mounds of bread were baked every morning; several flaps of it accompanied every meal. Or *were* the meal: for breakfast we had bread dipped in olive oil, then dipped in a mix of dried oregano, salt and paprika for flavouring, washed down with several glasses of sweet tea.

"Sheep, Yan, come here," Alia said after breakfast, heading out into the desert with a plastic bucket. Umm Tahir had clearly taken against me in the night: she'd done nothing but glower at me through breakfast. But she did have a lot of children to feed and fuss over, all of whom were having varying degrees of morning tantrums; I was something for Alia to deal with.

It was milking time and everyone was involved, except Rathwan. Alia laughed and pointed to him as we passed his part of the tent: there he was, unashamedly fast asleep under a pile of blankets.

"Rathwan, sleeping, sleeping always."

Not for the first time or the last, I wondered if he had something wrong with him to need so much sleep. Perhaps he expended more energy than the rest of us when he was awake, given his performance-level conversation and constant eye to the main chance. Or perhaps he just didn't like to be awake for anything that might be menial work.

There were a lot of sheep and goats; all personnel over the age of six knew what to do with them and were supervised by Rathwan's father and his shepherd. The shepherd was a young Syrian who looked like an ethnically accurate picture of Jesus – handsome, bearded and dark. He added to his Jesus-likeness by riding on the back of a small donkey as he brought the flocks in from the desert hills.

There was a flurry of shouting, stick-waving, whistling and stone-throwing to round the animals into an orderly group. (A tip: if you ever need to head off a fleeing sheep, throw a stone just in front of it and it turns back.) The toddlers ran in and out of the animals in a fooling-around imitation of the adults and bigger children. I tried to look useful but wasn't.

The tricky bit, once you've got your flock contained, is to rope them up for milking. They were fastened into long rows, each one facing in the opposite direction to the next – head, tail, head, tail and so on for yards. The milkers worked their way efficiently along both sides of the rows. Milking sheep looks easy: just pull on the two teats. But try as I might to copy Alia I couldn't get a squirt out of mine. Alia and the children found my determination and failure hilarious. Umm Tahir just looked at me with sneering impatience – no, as far as she was concerned I wasn't funny at all. I ignored her and provoked more hilarity from Alia and Yousef by pronouncing my sheep defective.

"Yes, yes," Alia said. "Yan's sheep is bad."

They were all bad, actually, bad, demanding beasts. Neither the sheep nor the goats seemed to yield much milk for all the work involved: at the end of the session, we had just one small milk churn, not quite full, from the sheep, and one barely a quarter-full from the goats. Sheep were more valuable than goats, but in my opinion both animals could try a bit harder to merit their reputation for usefulness. Dead they were good. Dead they were wool and cloth and meat, but alive they were just having a laugh.

The con-tricksters were released from their bonds, brought to order and escorted back up to the hills by the shepherd and little Yousef. The milking happened every morning and late afternoon. I never mastered the art of it but I didn't tire of finding the process exciting. One afternoon I watched Rathwan's father: he'd seen all this happen twice a day just about every day of his life, yet I saw a thrill of joy in his expression – the desert, his flocks, his cavorting children, everything he wanted spread out in front of him for him to delight in. Whatever the Arabic is for 'This is the life', he was thinking it.

But it was obviously not the life for Rathwan. He was still asleep when we came back to the tent. As I went into the kitchen with Alia, Umm Tahir and the toddlers, I saw his father heave a sigh and go to wake Rathwan with a firm shake.

We were busy in our part of the tent. There was much refurbishment work on the children: they were swiftly and thoroughly scrubbed down in a large plastic bowl filled with water heated in a can over the fire. Their hair was washed with a bar of soap and there were squawks when the suds got in their eyes; but the production line was soon done and clean clothes put on them before they'd a chance to let out a full complaint.

Apart from on special occasions, Bedouin children wear cheap, colourful Western clothes – far easier to deal with in a hand-wash than the yards of traditional cotton robes. The littlest ones were washed and changed frequently; using cloth nappies would have been just as much work and disposable ones would have created a hideous litter across the desert (where a family of five children is thought to be on the small side). Bedouin children sometimes look a lot poorer than they are, simply because it's so hard to keep them clean; in the dust of the desert, a grimeless hour would be good going. What might at first glance look like a gang of scruffy urchins are healthy, well nourished and have been in recent contact with soap.

Once they'd been washed, the two little girls, Timani and Radya, tottered outside in their clean frocks. I went to see what they were up to: among the chickens, picking up bits of interesting-looking cardboard rubbish off the ground and eating them. My first instinct made me take the delicious rubbish off them, saying "No. Dirty." Then I realised this was crazy: these children lived outside – if anything, I'd be preventing them from building up a natural resistance to minor stomach bugs. Although hands and dishes were constantly, ferociously washed, there was no way tent life could be as surgically clean as Western child-rearing demanded. All those terrifying adverts with babies crawling across germ-ridden kitchen floors, bound to die if the right germ-killing detergent hasn't been applied hourly to all surfaces – were we bringing up healthy children or making money for the manufacturers? Building up a robust tolerance to dirt was exactly what Timani and Radya needed to be doing. As if realising that

I'd work this one out for myself, the girls found more rubbish to eat and tip-tottered rapidly back to their mother, away from the silly, interfering blonde person.

Rathwan had been mustered from his pit and appeared in the cooking section looking very smart in a navy-blue suit. Even a tie. He told me that as it was the feast day, he had to go to the village with his father to visit friends and relatives.

"They will all be men so I have to leave you here for a few hours. I will tell Alia to look after you."

"No don't, or she'll think I'm a pain. I'll be fine."

"I'll just tell Alia to let you watch what she does. I'll tell her the work is interesting to you."

"We're all right. Don't start bossing everyone around on my behalf."

He laughed quietly and asked how I was getting on with Umm Tahir, in a way that told me one would be expected not to get on with her.

"I'm fine. Go."

He looked a little hurt at my prickly independence. I tried to soften up a little. "You look nice. I've never seen you in a suit."

"It's a special occasion." Then, apologetically, he added, "Some old women will be coming later. Do you have a skirt?"

I had one.

"It should be a long skirt."

"It's ridiculously long. Go."

He dithered, thinking I might be annoyed about the skirt business or feeling neglected by him. A car horn was tooting. Despite my orders, he said something bossy-sounding to Alia.

I rolled my eyes for her benefit: "Go away, Rathwan, leave us alone."

Alia laughed and found a suitable English phrase from her schooldays: "Rathwan, shut your mouth."

"*Aiwa*," I said. That's right. Rathwan retreated with much exaggerated tutting and head-shaking.

He'd told me that a sheep or a goat would be slaughtered for the feast and the traditional Bedouin dish *mensaf* prepared from the meat. I'd imagined this slaughtering would be some sort of ritual and hoped I wouldn't spoil my manners by coming over squeamish or passing out as a huge glinting sword slit open the terrified beast to a chorus of devout prayers. But when I returned from another visit to my cave, I found Alia had unceremoniously cut the throat of a young sheep round the back of the tent and was pulling the skin off as it lay in a pool of blood. She then disembowelled it as briskly as she had kneaded the bread dough, cut off its head and hung the carcass up from the tent ropes to drain the remaining blood.

The entrails were fried with onions – this was clearly a little pre-feast treat for the women and children, but having watched Alia squeeze droppings out of the animal's intestines, I found it difficult to face these particular organs lightly browned on the end of a fork. The head was boiled and some grotesque inner matter dug out of it for eating. Its eyes were already missing by this stage. I wondered if it was a Western myth that the eyes were considered the best bit and fed to an honoured guest. Not me, necessarily, I wasn't insulted to be a lower sort of guest unworthy of eyes, no, not at all . . . But I didn't see anyone else get them.

I suspected if anyone had them it was Umm Tahir, she was the sort to gobble down the best bit and blame it on me.

I racked my brain for ways to stave off Umm Tahir's growing resentment and irritation, but I've never been a great disemboweller – not much of a dab hand in the kitchen at all, let alone useful with charcoal fires and entrails. I tried to spot something that needed doing and that I could possibly do, but it was always done better and faster before I got there. So I sat around trying to look willing and pleasant but achieving nothing. Of course I was irritating – this useless thing, loafing around, grinning inanely, couldn't even string a sentence together to explain itself.

Seeing her point of view, I gave up on Umm Tahir and stuck to Alia like I was tattooed on her. She didn't mind me. Usually no one paid much attention to Alia as she drudged through her day; having someone watch her fascinated, obeying her orders, holding things they were told to hold and moving when instructed, was a diverting novelty for her. Alia was cheerful, hard-working and unfailingly obedient. She would hunch herself up slightly, as if hoping not to be noticed as anything other than a useful piece of household equipment. But somewhere in her sardonic eyes and occasional tone of voice was a person saying, "You think all this doesn't drive me crazy?"

If the tale about the sheep's eyes was one of our myths, I later came across what I thought might be a Bedouin women's myth about Western girls. When I went to change into my skirt in preparation for the arrival of the guests, Alia came with me to what had been our bedroom. Now the mattresses had been arranged neatly around the sides of the tent, with cushions placed on them to make comfortable seats for the visitors. The plastic floor-covering had been swept and my suitcase tidily stowed on the small trunk that was Alia's wardrobe. As I opened my case, Alia was pretending to be absorbed in rearranging her white head scarf, but she had one curious eye on me all the time. I opened my case wide to show I didn't mind if she wanted to look at my things; her life had been on show to me all morning.

I changed into an ankle-length skirt and long-sleeved top, thinking that I looked quite demure enough for the severest old lady visitor. But Alia seemed concerned, asking me an urgent question. When I didn't understand, she pulled up her dress – and under a few other layers of dress and a pair of leggings, she showed me that she was wearing good, solid interlock knickers. Knickers straight out of an Enid Blyton fourth-former's wardrobe: a sensible, netball-captain's navy-blue. I showed her mine. Barely knickers at all compared to hers, but she seemed reassured if a little surprised. I had a very powerful feeling from her reaction that the Bedouin had a story going round about Western girls not wearing any. I was pleased to have saved our reputation.

Rathwan and his father returned with the guests. I barely saw them before I was closeted away with the female visitors: a small old woman in black and her tall, severely black-clad daughter, Fatima. Fatima was very pale and clear-skinned, the way nuns from enclosed orders look, spared spots and wrinkles for their blessedness. Her black head scarf framed her face like a nun's veil but there was something shrill about her around the eyes that told you this was no sweet, twittering innocent from the chorus of *The Sound of Music*.

The old woman was Umm Tahir's mother and Fatima was her sister. Afterwards, Rathwan quizzed me about the old woman, worried she might have been unfriendly and disapproving. But she was perfectly sweet to me, appreciative of any effort I made throughout the long afternoon to say a few words in Arabic; and when I stood up, she looked at my skirt, saw that it reached my ankles and nodded approvingly.

Fatima had been the trouble. All afternoon she'd shared whispered, smirking conversations with Umm Tahir, both of them looking right at me. There was nothing I could do except give them my toughest sneer, trying to indicate that if I weren't on my best behaviour I'd slap them. The sneer didn't seem to translate: they carried right on.

After the men had eaten, the *mensaf* was brought through for us. The others helped themselves from a large central platter, using their right hands, but Umm Tahir brought me a spoon and a small plate of my own. This may have been out of consideration for my different eating habits but, more likely, it was a way of keeping my paws out of the communal dish; Westerners are thought unclean and many Muslims prefer not to eat from the same plate.

Mensaf is delicious: tender meat in a rich, tangy sauce of yoghurt and pine nuts, served on a bed of saffron rice. Unfortunately, there's something about the combination that makes more than the smallest portion swell inside me and edge me towards throwing up. *Mensaf* is what the Old Testament tells good Jews they shouldn't eat – a kid seethed in its mother's milk. It certainly seethes inside me.

I decided that throwing up would be more ungracious than pretending to have a small appetite. Luckily, everyone else was in such an eating fever they didn't notice what I was up to as I slipped most of my portion back onto the main platter.

The *mensaf* was followed by sweets, oranges, tea and ages of sitting around. The afternoon was passing by. "This is my life passing by," I thought, as yet another desultory conversation passed me by. Suddenly we had a change of pace. Activity. Umm Tahir was showing off her dresses, bringing out at least a dozen from her part of the tent – blue, crimson, green, velvets, velours, satins, all yoked with rich embroidery or stiff with sequins. We were supposed to coo and stroke them admiringly as she held them up against herself, preening and prancing. I was a very reluctant sycophant at the court of Queen Umm Tahir but gasped praises along with the rest.

All of an out of the blue, Fatima pulled at my shirt. At first I thought she was trying to attract my attention, then I realised she was pulling it to see if I had anything on underneath. I was glad I'd put on a T-shirt under the long-sleeved shirt: modesty itself. Umm Tahir smirked at me and their mother told Fatima off – but she didn't seem much chastened. When Alia and I had had the knicker show, it just made me laugh. This made me furious. And I was furious for not having any words to express my fury. I got up, nodded politely at the old woman and walked out.

I didn't go far: just round to the back of the tent, where dried blood was baking into the sand and bits of sheep skin swarmed with flies. I was sick of sitting in the tent anyway, all the sun and fresh air going to waste in claustrophobic pettiness. I stood and watched the calming desert. There was another tent out there, could have been half a mile away. It had camels tethered near it; not such a common sight in the Eastern Desert. Rathwan said four-wheel drives were more practical; camels were slower and far more wayward. Some Bedouin liked to have a few around, like prize pets, symbols of the spirit of a way of life surviving even though a Toyota and a Merc were parked alongside them. Across the distance, one of the camels set up their terrible, off-key roaring. I wished I'd been able to produce a sound like that and done it loud in Fatima's face.

"Yan, come here." Alia was standing behind me. I told myself to grow up and follow her back in. I hadn't been long; for all anyone knew, I'd only been to the toilet.

Mercifully, the guests were leaving. I shook Fatima's hand, looked her in her rather attractive face and said quietly, with a warm smile, "May you grow as ugly as your nature."

We went through to sit with Rathwan and his father, but a few moments later another visitor, a man, arrived. I rose to leave, but Rathwan's father motioned me to sit down again.

"This man is an old friend of the family, like an uncle. My father invites you to stay here."

The way the visitor looked at my ankles didn't seem very avuncular to me. I shifted round to sit on my feet, but Uncle's eyes merely re-focused on my chest. He was probably in his early fifties, fat and with ratty eyes. I think I'd been kept there to amuse him, because after a brief introduction of me and my motives, Father laughed and said, "If you are not married, my friend says he is looking for a new wife."

"Thank you," I replied, "but I'm not looking for a husband today."

This was greeted with guffaws. Rathwan, who was translating, was taking the conversation less in his stride than I was.

"He has camels." Now this I don't believe I heard for real: "He will give your father all his camels for you."

"What will my father do with camels? He flies aeroplanes."

"Camels like to go in aeroplanes, they like to see the world."

"So do I. I'd be a very bad wife, never at home."

"He doesn't mind. He likes you."

Rathwan was getting extremely twitchy. Keeping a fixed grin, he muttered to me, "This man is stupid. See how he stares at you? He's not joking."

"It's all right," I muttered back. "It's harmless."

Rathwan's father was looking at me thoughtfully. "So, your father is alive?"

"Yes."

He looked still more thoughtful. I suppose if my father were like him, I wouldn't be allowed to gad about the world taunting old men.

"What is your education?"

I told them I'd been to university. They asked why I wasn't married. Rathwan explained that customs were very different in the West, where people married much later in life. Uncle then told us that he had six children but wanted to catch up with Rathwan's father. I wished him luck.

"But I need a new wife for this, a strong new wife."

His father said something that really made Rathwan lose his

sense of humour. He wouldn't translate it.

"Just ignore it. This remark is not worth repeating."

I pestered him to tell me.

"OK. He said that in this country, if a woman is not pregnant six months after the wedding, they take her to the doctor."

More than insensitive of a man who'd divorced Rathwan's mother for not having enough children. In all his affability, it was easy to forget that Rathwan's father was not an entirely nice man.

The older men moved on to another topic, but Uncle kept watching me all the time. Rathwan asked me how things had gone 'on the other side'. As I recounted my afternoon to Rathwan, with Uncle's ratty eyes fixed on me, I suddenly began to see the attraction of 'the other side'.

"I'm tired," I told Rathwan. "I'm going next door."

"I think you're right."

My bedroom section was empty. Reprieved from minding my manners and looking eager, I lay down with a book and felt looseness come creeping into muscles that seemed to have been standing at attention all day.

But Tahir, a boisterous six-year-old, came galloping in and flung himself down beside me. I wasn't in the mood to humour him. He'd struck me as being extremely spoilt, with a tendency to push the smaller kids over and run off leaving them bawling. His mother's son. He watched me for a while; I ignored him. He said something that sounded like language he shouldn't be using at his age and stomped off. He'd probably give Timani and Radya a good kicking to cheer himself up.

I was reading about Gertrude Bell for the first time. When she

115

travelled in the Middle East, she was treated as an honorary man; she had almost nothing to do with the women of Arabia. I knew it was good that the world had moved on, that a Western woman in Jordan had no special status and was just one of the girls. But I wasn't exactly that either. Unlike a respectable Jordanian woman, I could be stared at and sniggered over because . . . well, because everyone knew what foreign girls were like: no knickers, you know. It wasn't easy being one of the girls, wearing what convention dictated I should wear, sitting where convention told me I should sit; I couldn't remember ever having to obey so many rules. But I'd bitten my tongue and accepted the conventions, only to find that they didn't reward me by enfolding me in their protection.

"The man has gone," Rathwan came in. "Are you all right?"

"Yes, I just wanted to read my book. Are you all right?"

He wasn't. He rubbed at his forehead, tired and agitated.

"Sometimes my father . . . He speaks and doesn't think."

Didn't think much about Rathwan and Alia; that was becoming obvious. I held Rathwan's hand and squeezed it. "I know."

"You can come back now and sit with me if you like."

"I will."

Alia came in. I dropped Rathwan's hand but she'd seen. Rathwan smiled at her, put his finger to his lips and went out.

"Yan," Alia said, sitting down next to me, looking at me with new interest. "Rathwan good."

"Yes."

She was pleased. She jumped back on her feet. "Come here, Yan, tea."

We carried the tea through to Rathwan and his father. It was television time. The black-and-white set was kept boxed up in its protective polystyrene moulding and was liberated at the same time every evening. An hour of news. Then a bizarre programme of military displays interspersed with messages home from Jordanian boys who were with the peacekeeping forces in Croatia. We'd see film of them saying "Hello, Mum" and looking cheery, then see Mum or Dad or forty brothers, sisters and cousins not looking cheery. Then other film would cut in of swashbuckling activity with swords and horses on a parade ground in Jordan. Or there were foot soldiers who didn't just march past the camera – they danced, they chanted, they clapped rhythms in unison at the speed of machine-gun fire. I had a suspicion that the Jordanian army was mainly for show – but what a show.

Top television events for the girls were the Egyptian soap operas that were shown for hours every night. Alia and Umm Tahir watched spellbound as jewel-bedecked women bumped into the scenery and milked every emotion like . . . well, if they'd been milking sheep instead, there'd have been a good churnful every five minutes. Eternal love polygons abounded. All the men were terrifyingly ugly, the women so shoulder-padded and heavily made up that they looked like drag queens.

As everything was so overstated, I found the programmes quite useful for picking up Arabic. The commercials were rather less useful: hideous jangling jingles, sung by gaggles of simpering pubescent girls as they skipped idiotically around one of Jordan's ancient monuments. There was a determined campaign for a brand of tissues called Fine. Obviously these weren't 'women's tissues', although it was always young women who would be agog with joy to be handed a box of them. I don't know why they were so delighted, because the tissues seemed to have no practical function except to be waved around in their box while the girls sang "Fine, Fine, Fine." I could sing you the jingle now if you wanted, it was so irritatingly memorable, but you'd be sorry you asked.

An advert for a Cornetto-like ice cream had even more alarming music: Beethoven's Fifth, just those famous first bars, played on Arab instruments – da da da dum, twangety twang, da da da dum. Beethoven's Cornetto ad went on for a very long time and featured a woman who wore a different outfit in every frame and wandered about posh hotel foyers, chatting charmingly to a man we could only hope was her husband. It ended with her and the man in a pedalo, looking suspiciously post-coital and smug, eating ice cream and heading away from the sunset and towards the camera, closer and closer, looming horrendously large – it cut just before they hit the lens.

The evening's television viewing was interrupted by the arrival of more male visitors. Us girls were irritated at having to scuttle off just as one of the drag queens was lurking in wait for her villainous husband with a sharp letter-opener. Not wanting a riot in the women's quarters – or to meet with a nasty letter-opener accident himself – Rathwan's father turned the set round so that we could watch it through the entrance to our section. No peace for the wicked though: Umm Tahir was soon summoned to trot to and fro with reheated *mensaf* for the guests. Uncharacteristically, she put platefuls in front of Alia and me. In the soap opera, a sub-plot drag queen was busy poisoning her sister's food.

Father had gone. After the morning milking, he'd driven off in his truck and wouldn't be back until the following day. He'd taken the second wife's two older sons with him; a shame really, just when I was beginning to figure out what their names were.

"He has to see his other wife," Rathwan explained. "Umm Tahir will be in a very bad mood."

But Umm Tahir was as happy as a teenage girl with a brand-new box of Fine, Fine, Fine. Everyone was, as if a weight had been lifted from us. We could be where we wanted to be in the tent, we could laugh loudly, jump, shout, run about and not worry if our ankles were showing.

Umm Tahir was so skittishly not in a bad mood, she collected her children and went out visiting. I'd been so busy sulking the previous day, I hadn't noticed a small tent a few hundred yards away, at the end of the cart track that led past ours. Or perhaps they'd just arrived, our new next-door neighbours. Next-flap neighbours.

Little Yousef was off on sheep and goat duties with the Syrian. I could see the two of them on the side of a nearby hill. I would have thought shepherding would be fairly easy: a lot of lolling against a rock thinking your thoughts, interrupted only by milking and the occasional patrol to check no lambs had fallen down holes . . . I could be a shepherd perhaps, out in the sun, writing a novel to the sound of gentle baaing and tinkling goat

119

bells . . . I'd have been in fairly short-term employment: watching Yousef and the Syrian, I realised they worked incessantly. The beasts had to be kept in a neat formation on a particular patch of hillside, presumably to regulate the grazing area as well as prevent hole-falling. Precision stone-throwing, running, stick-brandishing, whistling – you'd be lucky to get a postcard written.

Rathwan and Alia were talking in low, serious tones in the tent. It sounded as if she was telling him her problems, so I left them to it and made free in the kitchen while Umm Tahir wasn't around to be put out. I heated some water, took the plastic bowl through to what I thought of as my bedroom and gave myself a sort of bath. I even shaved my legs – all the stuff there was usually no privacy to do. Women could be kept out of the front part of the tent, but our three sections served as a thoroughfare for all the family. Tent life was designed to keep people well behaved. No locked doors to sin behind; a child could come barrelling through a flap or a father come looking for a child at any moment . . .

I put in some hard work with cleansers and moisturisers – just in the nick of time before Rathwan noticed that after a couple of days without the customary maintenance I looked like a potato in a wig.

In the Sinai Desert, my Australian friends and I had slept out under the stars after a day-long camel trek. At first light, while everyone sensible was still asleep, I sat up in my sleeping bag, did all my duties with cleansers and moisturisers, then applied my mascara, eyeliner and lipstick. The girl beside me opened one eye, watched me for a moment, then said, "Now that has to be the definition of vanity."

Yes, I was demented, a mad monstress of vanity – couldn't help myself. I turned my attention to my hair – matted up like an old goat's. But this wasn't vanity: a person could go bald if they didn't wash their hair. Wasn't that a scientific fact?

Alia and Rathwan had become aware of my antics with bowls and jugs.

"What are you doing?"

"Nothing. I'm going to wash my hair."

"Good idea."

So he had noticed its goatishness.

"Thank you."

He grinned. "I'll help you."

We went to the side of the tent where there was nothing but desert ahead of us. I knelt down. Rathwan brought jugs of warm water. In the near silence, he slowly washed my hair for me. It felt like a biblical anointing: the water trickling gently over my head, the cautiously light touch of his hands. A soft breeze over the warm desert caressed us as I felt every care I ever had slip away from me, leaving a new soul at perfect peace.

The Syrian shepherd came round the corner of the tent and gasped in horror at the sight of us. Rathwan laughed. "The spell is broken."

Umm Tahir brought a friend home for lunch, a woman from the tent up the tracks. She had blue eyes, light-brown hair and pale skin. She'd seen me and wanted to meet this similar-looking oddity.

Why did an Arab woman look like her? It could be she was one of the Circassians, Sunni Muslims from the Caucasus who fled to Jordan from Russian persecution at the end of the nineteenth century. They helped create the city of Amman, which was not much more than an abandoned collection of Roman ruins when they arrived. As they tended to be an urban people, they rarely intermarried with the nomadic Bedouin; around Amman and the town of Jerash, their light colouring was not an unusual sight. Then again, the Circassians were only one of the many swathes of immigration or conquest to mingle blood with Jordan's Arab tribes over thousands of years of history. Our neighbour's looks could come from a time before time was measured in any way we'd recognise.

Anyway, she was friendly, Muna from next door.

"She loves you," Alia said. "You are beautiful."

I thanked Muna for this rush of affection and told her she was beautiful too.

"No," Alia translated, "you biggest very beautiful." Even Umm Tahir was nodding.

Well, being a walking definition of vanity, I was finding this a very pleasant way to spend the lunch hour.

Muna suddenly grabbed hold of my bare calf and squeezed it. Then she pulled up her skirt and leggings to show me her own slim calves. Umm Tahir hitched up her skirts as well and displayed a dark, lean leg worthy of a model, but the admiring fuss over my legs continued. Muna's skin was pale, so the colour of mine wasn't their selling point. I was a very different build to the Arab women: years of cycling and weightlifting had left me quite heftily muscled, in a way I frequently regretted. That was what it was:

"Beautiful," Alia exclaimed. "Yan, beautiful *food* in the legs."

In the late afternoon, a dry storm got up; sand and dust blew into the tent and the wind was tearing at its fabric. Alia ran about with a bowl of water, sprinkling the ground by all the tent's entrances, fervently muttering something. I thought she was performing some sort of traditional anti-hurricane ritual and prayers.

"What's she doing? What's she doing?"

Rathwan looked surprised at my lack of common sense.

"If the ground is wet there's less dust."

"But what's she saying? Why's she muttering like that?"

"She's swearing about the dust."

Soon there was more to swear about. Part of the tent collapsed in the swelling gale and only an hour's blast with a fireman's hose would have kept the dust down. Chickens were running into the bedroom, children were crying, every inch of the tent was shaking and the no leg sheep was bawling pitifully. I realised poor little Yousef was still out in the hills; I wanted Rathwan to bring him back home.

"He'll be fine. He'll get behind a rock."

"He might be scared. I think we should go and get him."

"Really, there's no need. This doesn't last."

And at that very moment, like he was King of the Winds, the storm dropped to a light breeze, crying stopped, flapping flaps settled and the no leg sheep wound down to a whimper.

Umm Tahir gathered in dust-stuck children's clothes for re-washing. The King of the Winds helped Alia and me take the plastic floor-covering, cushions and mattresses outside to shake them out. I soon noticed that it was Alia and me doing the wrist-wrenching work of shaking, while the King of the Winds merely passed things to us and put them back. And he was handing them out faster than we could shake them.

"Hold on, hold on!" I snapped. "It's all right for you, this is hard work."

"*This* is hard work," he protested, the way five-year-olds tell lies, thinking the lie itself is the point, not believability.

"All right – swap with Alia then."

"No," he laughed. "Alia is not qualified to do this job. This job needs many qualifications."

"Rathwan, shut your mouth." Alia said.

We found that the shaking was more entertaining done to the rhythm of a song we started to the 'Fine, Fine, Fine' tune, with "Rathwan, shut your mouth" as the lyrics. Holding mattresses between us, Alia and I danced round and round, jumping high in the air on every second beat, bellowing our musical creation. Rathwan seized a cushion in each hand and shook them out with his arms held high, his feet stamping in the traditional Arab male dance. The singing and dancing completely took over from the work: Alia grabbed a plastic water can and beat out a rhythm on it, I sang "Rathwan, shut your mouth" and clapped, while Rathwan sang "Alia and Annie are horrible" to some tune of his own. Tahir ran over and danced around Alia. Timani and Radya trundled into our midst and did that insane running on the spot accompanied by over-excited, high-pitched screams toddlers world-wide seem to mistake for dancing and singing. As we worked ourselves into a dervish-like frenzy, Rathwan exploded with laughter, stopped his antics, threw an arm round my shoulder, kissed my cheek and said, "What will I do without you?"

Umm Tahir had just appeared in our part of the tent, curious to see if her children were being tortured, I expect. She took in the arm round me, the kiss, the whole thing. Rathwan hurried off with his cushions; Umm Tahir continued to hold my gaze. Then she smiled and nodded slowly. Now she'd got it.

I wouldn't say we became bosom friends after that, but she lost her worry that I was a sexual loose cannon; given that her husband was wealthy enough to take on more wives, it didn't do to have unspoken-for females sitting chatting to him. But now she knew I was very much spoken for. Besides, I was being useful for a change. She kept smiling at me as we shook out the rest of the mattresses together and laughed with me when Radya and Timani picked up a cushion between them and imitated us, shaking so forcefully they fell over.

As soon as all the cushions were back in place, Rathwan threw himself down on them.

"Oh, I am exhausted."

Alia and I exchanged a look.

"*Kaslaan*," Alia said

"Very," I said.

"How do you know what this means?" Rathwan asked. "You don't speak Arabic."

"No, but it's interesting that one of the few words I do know is the word for 'lazy'. It's also interesting that *kaslaan* rhymes with Rathwan."

A pause while he contemplated this. "Actually," he said, "you are not pronouncing it correctly."

Alia looked at me questioningly.

"Rathwan very bad," I said.

"Rathwan may be bad, but you are worse," he said, and closed his eyes.

We'd no time to bandy any more words with the likes of him. The fallen-down tent section needed putting back up and a tear in the canvas had to be sewn together. I held the canvas in place while Alia stitched, using a thick needle, wool yarn and a sharp-edged stone for scissors. Making as much noise as we could to disturb Rathwan, we heaved the wooden pole that supported the mended section back into place. On the final heave we fell back on the mattresses, laughing.

"Oh, Yan," Alia groaned, shaking her arms. "The hands, Yan, the hands tiring." Then she pointed to her feet with a laugh. "And legs tiring, Yan. The hands, the legs tiring."

I nodded. "Yes. Sheep, goats, bread, tent. Tiring."

She smiled wryly. "Yes, Yan. Yes."

Umm Tahir was calling her from the kitchen. Alia's face darkened and she sighed wearily.

"The head, Yan, tiring the head." And she pointed to her heart.

"Your sister has a tough life," I said, sitting down beside Rathwan. He opened his eyes.

"I know. I am thinking of something to organise that will make her happy."

"I hope so."

"Don't talk about it any more. It makes me sad. Tell me, what is this book you are reading?"

I told him about Gertrude Bell, showed him maps of where she'd travelled to, explained how the existence of Jordan had been partly her doing – all the ins and outs of her life that I could remember, up to her lonely suicide in Baghdad.

Rathwan sat bolt upright, horrified. "No! Don't tell me that."

"She did. She killed herself."

"That's terrible," he said, as if he were a close personal friend hearing the news for the first time. As I'd finished the book, he began to read it, sometimes asking me the meaning of words as he concentrated fiercely – *orchestrate, couture* . . .

I started reading Gertrude's own account of her travels, *The Desert and the Sown*; I found her hearty head-girl tone of voice alternately irritating and sad in its effort. I don't know where everyone one else had gone but we sat for hours with our books, exchanging the occasional flurry of remarks, like a comfortable old married couple. We would go, we decided, to all the places Gertrude had been.

"She will be our project," Rathwan said.

I agreed. "One day I'd like to see her house in Baghdad."

"Baghdad," Rathwan sighed. "I hear it is very beautiful. One day we'll be able to go together. *Inshallah.*"

The free-and-easy atmosphere continued through the evening. Rathwan and I went on with our reading; Yousef, in from the hills at last, curled up with his big brother, who showed him the pictures in his book and explained them to him. There was a comforting wood fire, chicken and rice for dinner, a sheepskin rug over the babies sleeping beside me. We'd tied down the tent flaps so they'd be secure against the newly rising wind. At the hour for the Egyptian soap operas, Alia made so bold as to bring her bread dough through to the front section and kneaded it half-heartedly while staring at the screen.

When Umm Tahir came in to watch television, her face was covered in a thick oily substance. Despite the rigours of her life, Umm Tahir had beautifully soft, clear skin. When I saw her oil-coated face, I thought there must be an ancient, secret, Bedouin women's recipe for a perfect complexion. I'd find out what it was and . . . Well, eat your heart out, Anita Roddick.

After much signalling, Umm Tahir finally understood my enquiry. She went to the kitchen and came back with a tin of Vaseline.

Perhaps because I'd stayed up later, enjoying the relaxed atmosphere, I woke the next morning to find that I'd missed milking. Everyone was in agitated discussion in the front of the tent. I fled to and from my cave, washed and started sorting out something clean to put on. Alia came in wearing her best frock – faded black velvet with a slightly fraying embroidered yoke. She looked very excited.

"Yan, come here." She motioned me through to the front.

"Annie," Rathwan said. "We are going with Alia to visit my aunt. The one we saw in the bank. My father will give us a lift now if you're ready."

Barely awake, I certainly wasn't ready.

"Now?" I asked crossly. "But I want to change my clothes. I need some time."

"Please," Rathwan said quietly, "we have been waiting for

you. He wants to go now."

"If I'd known this was going to happen I'd have been ready. Why didn't you tell me before?"

His father was watching me with alarm and said something to Rathwan.

"My father says you are welcome to stay here if you prefer, but I have to be with Alia or she won't be allowed to go."

I saw the tinge of worry in Alia's excitement and realised I was being a brat. This outing was the 'something' Rathwan had organised to make his sister happy.

"No, tell him I'm fine. I was just confused. I'll be one minute."

I changed shirts, grabbed my bag and hurried to join them in the Toyota. Rathwan's father owned three vehicles. As well as the Toyota four-wheel drive, there was a huge, brightly painted open lorry that was used for transporting all the family's belongings when the tent was moved to another site, usually every six months. Then there was a contraption down in the milking area that looked like an oil tanker but was actually full of water for the flocks.

The Bedouin took what they found useful from the modern world but the essence of their lives remained the same. Even television-watching seemed to only fulfil curiosity, not tilt the certainty that they knew best. For the men, it was a life of vigorous boy-scouting serviced by dutiful women; why give up that freedom to pay bills and worry about un-needful possessions? Perhaps the 'Fine, Fine, Fine' girls and the Egyptian drag queens made the women's heads turn, but where would they go with their ideas in a spin? What would

Alia do if she ran away with just loose change in her pocket? How could tent-bound Alia ever meet an Arabic-speaking Westerner who'd take care of her in Europe? How could she find the confidence to believe that she'd probably survive, honour intact, no matter where she ran off to? Or come to believe that honour mattered less than curiosity satisfied? Even if she was tired in her hands and her heart, the community she was brought up in had made sure that girls like Alia lived in holy terror of the world outside.

Rathwan's tattooed aunt had left the desert for a rambling house on the fringe of Amman but she still kept her rooms stripped bare of all but the essentials, filling them instead with children and Bedouin tradition. I was ready for Auntie, but she baulked to see the strange creature from the bank arriving through her front door, taking off its shoes and sitting itself down in her living room. But she clearly doted on Alia and Rathwan, was beside herself hugging and welcoming them. As I was in their charge I was welcomed too, once she'd got over the turn I'd given her. Not welcome, I suspected, was Rathwan's father, who'd dropped us off at the top of the road. I imagined history hadn't made him a fond figure for Auntie at all – he was the man who'd sent her sister away to a life of poverty with three young children.

The household was so different to life with Rathwan's father. Auntie had crowds of big daughters, chattering and laughing loud in every room – female presence dominated the house. They swooped on Alia and carried her off with them, gossiping, giggling and cuddling her. She was happier than I'd ever seen her; this was much more her family than any of the half-brothers and sisters at the tent.

The tall girl from the bank was wearing a bright red trouser suit and high black heels, her wavy hair tumbling over her shoulders. Nuha – stunning and self-possessed. She was asking me about myself in lilting English when her little mother started ushering her out of the door.

"Excuse me. We'll be back soon. I look forward to talking with you further."

"I expect they have to go shopping for groceries," Rathwan said, lying down on one of the mattresses that lined the walls of the room. "Oh, I am really exhausted."

I sat with him for a while as small cousins climbed over him and questioned him. The room was long and cool. It had two carpeted sections divided by a strip of bare concrete leading from the front door, where a flock of shoes were halted – dragging outside dirt inside was thus avoided. A little girl with short hair brought us tea; she was Lena, about ten years old and determined no one else would ever get to sit next to me but her. Meanwhile, two teenage boys, Ali and Isam, wanted to practise their English; I took out my Arabic phrasebook and a two-way lesson began. Rathwan's eyes were closing.

Suddenly, everything was thrown into disarray by the raucous arrival of a manic little boy with blue eyes and a blast of Harpo Marx blonde hair. He was running, yelling, somersaulting and pulling a tiny live bird on a string.

"What's this?"

"This is Rashid," Rathwan said. "He looks odd and he is odd."

Ali bellowed at Rashid. Rashid ignored Ali and continued running up and down the room, yelling and hauling the poor bird behind him. Ali snatched the bird away. Rashid let out a wail like an air-raid siren, kicking furiously at Ali's shins.

"Rashid!" everyone shouted. He banged out of the front door, crying and screaming terrible curses at us all, wailing all the way up the street and beyond. Ali untied the quaking little bird and put it on the outside window sill. It took a moment to collect itself before it flew off, fast.

"Rashid," Ali sighed, as he sat down rubbing his shins. Everyone shook their heads.

"Rashid is impossible," Rathwan laughed. "But I think people with this hair and eyes are born strange."

Before I could think of a riposte, he yawned.

"Really, I think I need to sleep for a while."

He peeled a small boy off himself and closed his eyes again. I was enjoying the atmosphere in this house and I wanted him to share it with me.

"Oh, don't sleep yet."

"I hate you," he said. He sat up and lit a cigarette. Then he spotted a way out: "You know, it is a very nice day. I will ask them to take you to the roof. You can see all the city from there and sunbathe."

With a cavorting train of cousins carrying mattresses, we went along a corridor to a yard at the rear where steps led up to the flat roof. A two-storey house: Auntie had done well for herself.

Once Rathwan had organised me in a comfortable spot, he edged to retreat: "It's too hot for me here. Send for me if you need me." He made his getaway before I could berate him.

Auntie's roof was halfway up one of Amman's seven hills; I could look down over similarly crowded roofs towards the city centre. Isam and Ali continued the Arabic-English lessons. There was some running up and down to ask Rathwan English words to surprise me with; I encouraged this practice until Ali returned with the sad news that Rathwan was asleep. He could pretend to be asleep better than anyone I knew.

Lena, and a friend she'd called up from the next door yard to look at me, sang me a song. I sang them a song. 'The Wild Rover' was the first one that came to mind, followed by whatever nursery rhymes I could remember. Every time I stopped, Lena clapped and shouted, *"Raneen, Yan, raneen!"* Sing, Anne, sing! We found common ground when I desperately got to "Christmas is coming, the goose is getting fat, please put a penny in the old man's hat." Lena and her friend had learnt it in their school English lessons; I wondered who thought that song was a halfway useful thing to teach Muslim children.

After a few hours of rooftop cabaret, Alia emerged from whatever she was up to with the older girl cousins. "Yan. Come here. Eat."

Auntie and Nuha had returned, prepared a feast and managed to stir Rathwan from his alleged sleep. We ate *mensaf* with several rounds of bread and side dishes of salads: green and red peppers chopped finely, humus, tahini, tomatoes with coriander, cucumbers and mint in yoghurt, rocket, radishes and olives. We had our own plates but there was no cutlery; Lena showed me how to use my bread as a neat scoop to serve myself from the central dishes.

Auntie's husband emerged for the first time; it was as if he was kept in some back room and only allowed out for meals. Like Rashid he had bright blue eyes, but they were ill matched with his dark, heavily wrinkled face. He looked tired and sick; the rowdy household obviously wore him out considerably more than it did his wife. He only ate a little, and Auntie fussed over him, urging him to eat more; but weariness and the racket of his children seemed to put him off swallowing more than a few mouthfuls. He spoke some English and told me that many years ago he'd had an English commanding officer in the army. Then he asked me if it was true that England was an island. I said it was. He said he'd heard this was the case. He went out of the room and came back with some photographs: his wife and himself when young, out in the desert by their flocks. Auntie was a pretty little slip of a girl, although she didn't seem herself without the tattoos; he'd looked careworn even then. His English ran out when I asked how long it had been since he'd left the desert.

Rathwan intervened. "Too long. He sold all his sheep and goats for this house. His wife has twelve children." There was some laughter. "He says thankfully now his wife is old and he can stop adding to the house."

Weary old Uncle retreated to wherever it was he hid from the bewildering female and child-domination of his life. Dinner was cleared away and Auntie moved to sit next to Rathwan, hugging him and whispering to him.

"My aunt wants me to get married. She thinks I should get married very soon. What do you think?"

"I think no one will have you."

He relayed this and Auntie ruffled his hair. "She says you're right. If I wait much longer I'll be useless."

Given her twelve children, I supposed Auntie must know best about men and their use-by dates.

"Of course," Rathwan added quietly, "I do know who I want to marry."

I saw Nuha understood this. I pretended I hadn't heard him.

Rathwan changed the subject. "I'm going to tell them some Bedouin stories and poems. It's a custom."

He began and held the whole room fascinated. He used a different accent for the recitations: more guttural and enunciated. They were old stories of desert battles, morality tales and poems of unrequited love. His voice was rhythmic and compelling – like listening to strange, gravelly music. It went on for about an hour; even Rashid curled up beside Ali, sucked his thumb and never moved his saucer eyes from Rathwan's face.

Along with everyone else, I was sorry when he stopped. But it was time for a gossip break. There was something Nuha wanted Rathwan to ask me.

"My cousin wants to know what you think about her situation. She's embarrassed her English is not good enough to explain but she's interested in your opinion. You see, she has been married but her husband was terrible. He beat her and she left him. Then she went back to him because she had a baby but now he has sent the baby away to his mother. He says he will give the baby to her if she gives him all her gold and wedding gifts."

I said I thought she was right to leave. "He's a bastard. Let him have the gold and choke on it." Nuha smiled and nodded. Auntie chipped in.

"My aunt wants me to go and see the husband for them."

"Yes, go and kick his head in."

The girls approved loudly of this suggestion. Rashid demonstrated effective head-kicking against a wall.

"It would be nice to do this but I think it will be better to negotiate. If he wants gold more than he wants his son, let him have it. But we must make sure that when it's negotiated, it is finished for good."

Everyone agreed with him, a little less enthusiastically than they'd agreed to the head-kicking. Poor Nuha, with her perfect, pale brown skin and deep, sad eyes. Best off home with Mum.

"What will happen to Nuha?" I asked Rathwan later. "Will she have to stay with her parents for good now?"

"No. I expect she will find another husband."

"Oh. I thought she'd be disgraced."

"In the old ways perhaps, but things are better now. She works in an office. She's clever and beautiful, she'll find a man who is sympathetic."

The next year I heard she was married to a sympathetic man and had her son safely with her. No one got kicked.

Alia and one of her girl cousins served us all with coffee.

Rathwan was excited: "We'll have coffee and Nuha will tell our fortunes. She has a great gift for this."

I suppose being in an exotic location, I'd expected something mystical, convincing even, but Nuha read our coffee grounds very much in the spirit of a parlour game. When it was Rathwan's turn, she said a great deal – but all he would tell me was that she'd said he would marry soon. I suspected something of a set-up there. When it came to my fortune, Nuha told me my cup was full of stories; there was a much-repeated message that someone loved me very much and that my eyes were full of tears.

"Why does she say this all the time?" Rathwan asked. "I only ever see you smiling or angry."

Nuha checked again: no, my eyes were definitely full of tears.

The fortune-telling moved on round the room but dissipated in noisy chat after Alia had been promised a husband in the near future. Who was the likely man? Many suggestions, much giggling and some tell-tale blushing from Ali, who left the room abruptly when he realised he'd betrayed his secret crush. More coffee, sweets, watermelon; Auntie even smoked one of my cigarettes and it didn't look like her first.

Rathwan told another Bedouin story. This time the steady rhythm of his voice put me to sleep. I woke when he gently shook my arm; the rest of the party was looking at me with concern.

"Oh, I'm sorry," I said. "How long was I asleep?"

"Just a few minutes. It's all right, everyone is tired now. Wait here and I'll see where you can sleep."

In one of the rooms off the corridor the floor was covered in mattresses made up with duvets and blankets, but against one wall stood a small single bed. Rathwan was helping Nuha and her sisters make up the bed for me. He fussed, plumped pillows and checked the corners were tucked in tight.

"Now," he said, "you will sleep well and be happy."

137

As usual, I worried that he'd been ordering people about on my behalf and had made them hate me – but that didn't seem to have happened. Lena had a jug of water for me; another cousin handed me a clean towel.

On the way to the bathroom, I encountered Rathwan's uncle. Wearing a woolly green tartan dressing gown over his traditional robes, he made a squeaking sound at me and shuffled rapidly past to wherever they kept him.

The bathroom was tiled and fully fitted out in avocado ceramics, right down to a bidet. But there was no running water – it had to be fetched from a huge barrel in the yard. Nevertheless, after my sordid cave, it was a 'Bathroom of Your Dreams' straight from a glossy magazine.

Nuha handed me a long blue nightdress and the bedroom was politely emptied for me to get changed. "Private," Nuha said, smiling, and closed the door behind her.

The moment I called to them that I was ready, the room was stormed by all the girls – and Rashid, who sneaked in sensing a promise of fun. Auntie sat cross-legged in the thick of it, her head uncovered and her long plaits hanging down either side of her face.

"*Raneen! Raneen!*" Lena urged me, and the others took up the chant. Groucho Marx's song 'Lydia the Tattooed Lady' leapt right to the front of my mind. I quickly pushed it way back again. But I could only remember a couple of lines of the few other songs that occurred to me; I resorted to repeating them over and over, hoping they'd think all English songs were lyrically stunted. I'd speed the lines up in each repetition, rising to a crescendo, trying to make it sound as if there was some sort of purpose to the musical tail-chasing. I worked up to quite a jaunty third repeat of the opening verse of 'Yesterday' and Lena started beating out a rhythm on an empty cake tin to spur me on. Everyone else clapped in time with her.

The clapping was like flamenco clapping, although the history probably ran from Arabia to Spain. The hands became instruments, not simply things to slap together in one unchanging beat – palms moved quickly across each other in complex, varying ways so the skin was its own drum. I sang on and on, repeating the words senselessly over the speeding beat. Much later on, I discovered that the repetition of a phrase which is considered beautiful is a feature of classical Arab song; so my performance probably seemed quite normal to the women.

I think I did my fragment of 'Yesterday' fifteen times before it got so fast my tongue tangled and I had to stop. Nuha brought in tea and Auntie produced a bag of pecan nuts from under her skirts – the night was young in the girls' dorm.

Lena's drumming started again and it was time for dancing. Rashid, only in on a temporary guest pass, didn't count, Auntie declined on the grounds of age, and when I saw what the others were doing, I declined on a plea of incompetence; actually, I was afraid of losing my New Cinderella. The girls swayed and clapped in a circle, each one taking the centre in turn. The centre dancer tied a red sash round her hips, then raised her arms in the air and shook those hips from side to side like they were going to fly right out of her body, some of the dancers reaching a speed that sent them into a blur. It was like fast, frantic belly-dancing:

just the thing if you were planning to strain your pelvis with twelve kids.

Auntie, Rashid and I cheered and clapped from the sidelines. Last and by far the best was Alia: she was the quickest, the most rollingly erotic. Her usually huddled physicality erupted into this powerful, sexy young woman, completely sure of herself and how good she was. A huge cheer went up. Alia flushed pink and delighted in the glory, then fell on her mattress exhausted. The dancing had done it for everyone; time for lights out.

The cousins changed for bed, expressing some amusement that Alia didn't – especially when they saw she even kept her head covered. Town mice and country mouse. They stopped talking about it when they saw she was upset. Lena took a scarf and wrapped it around her own head, pronouncing it an ideal way to sleep.

Rathwan was still sleeping in the front room when a huge breakfast was served. He woke up when Rashid, wearing a pair of ladies' evening gloves for reasons best known to himself, jumped onto him.

Rathwan pretended to be grouchy with me. "Oh, so how was the party last night? What a racket. I thought you were tired."

I told him what had been going on.

"Alia was the best? Really?"

"You've never seen her?"

"Of course not. This dancing isn't for men to see."

A friend of Auntie's gave us a ride back to Mafraq. The further we got from the aunt's house, the sadder Alia was, all her magnificence of the night before seeping out of her.

In Mafraq, half the shops were still shuttered up for Eid al Adhah.

"I'll get us a taxi," Rathwan said. He handed Alia some money. "Will you go with Alia? She needs to buy a new head scarf."

Alia brightened when we found a dress shop open. We dithered between a crimson scarf patterned with autumn leaves and a navy one with pale blue flowers. Perhaps to suit her mood, Alia chose the autumnal one. Her kind big brother was waiting for us in a taxi with a bag of bananas: a treat for me. He knew I could eat a treeful of them in a sitting. (My brother, who hates anything that might be a fruit or vegetable, has a theory that I'm not fully evolved.) I was going to ask Rathwan what Muslims think about evolution, but he was telling Alia one of his funny stories to cheer her up.

The taxi took us to the Bedouin village, and then our helpful desert patrolman dropped us at the tent. Alia was just in time to take off her finery and help with the afternoon milking.

"My father has something for you," Rathwan told me when milking was over. His father handed me a cloth-covered jerry can, talking to me in his disconcerting way, looking fixedly at me and never at Rathwan, who was providing all the translation.

"He notices you buy water in bottles. It's expensive for you. This is water from a fresh spring, the same as in the bottles."

His father became gruff and deprecating when he saw how touched I was. The Syrian was down at the tent for a meal break and wanted to know why I couldn't drink the ordinary water. It probably was ridiculous of me; I ate the food, I drank the tea, but I superstitiously avoided the water. I tried to explain in a way that wouldn't sound as though I thought their water was dirty. I said, fairly truthfully, that I only ever drank bottled water, even in London – especially in London.

The Syrian found this baffling. "Water is water. I drink the same water as the sheep and goats and it doesn't do me any harm."

Rathwan's father reacted with mock horror. "Oh my poor animals. If they're drinking the same water as you, they'll get sick. We'll have to take them to the hospital."

The Syrian laughed: "If they make it to the hospital."

Often the butt of this kind of teasing, the Syrian was nevertheless like family. (Although I never heard him addressed by name – he was always simply 'the Syrian'.) He came down to the tent to eat once a day, taking pocketfuls of bread back to the hills for his other meals. A shiny metal crook, a bed roll, a tobacco pouch and a water bottle seemed to be all he owned. During the day, he had Yousef or one of the older boys for company; at night, there were only the sheep and goats. Hardly surprising that he revelled in his bantering meal breaks, especially if there was a novelty act by the fire – the Syrian countryside wasn't exactly teeming with Westerners. He watched me with a sort of amazement, as if one of his goats was talking; but he would instantly lower his eyes if I looked back.

I knew there were rules about eye contact that I wasn't grasping. Although Rathwan's father stared at me when addressing me, he always looked away, almost confused, when I thought staring manfully back at him was the thing to do. Eyes down was Rathwan's etiquette tip when I checked with him, but it wasn't easy. I tried to make myself address his father with my eyes cast down, but it made me feel extremely vulnerable and my gaze would almost automatically spring back up; perhaps going up and down was only half as disrespectful.

Father was in a talkative mood the evening we came back from Auntie's, so my eyeline was all of a do. He scooped up little Radya and asked if I'd like to buy her; I said I would but I didn't think I could afford something so precious. Rathwan nodded at me: a good answer. Then his father asked me if we had black babies like this in England.

"Yes, some."

"Which are better, black babies or white babies?"

It was like him to ask this kind of question, testing me out. I'd have to find an answer that didn't sound as if I was putting down anything Jordanian but which didn't sound like intelligence-insulting crawling. For instance, when the Syrian had been complaining of a toothache, I'd been asked if I knew of a cure. I'd suggested cloves, an old emergency standby of my mother's, and Rathwan's father had looked contemptuous.

"Cloves? Do you think we don't have dentists?"

So I'd learnt to tread carefully. This time I said, "I think black babies are better – they don't show the dirt."

He roared with laughter, and ordered Yousef to bring us some tea. He asked me what other countries I'd been to, and pulled a face when I mentioned Egypt.

"Do you like Jordan or Egypt better?"

There he went again. Questions with potholes.

"Cairo is too crowded and the Bedouin I saw in Egypt were very poor."

"Yes. And the women are terrible. A friend of mine married an Egyptian woman and she nagged him all the time. Once he refused to tell her where he was going and she took off her shoes and beat him with them. Beat him with her shoes! What do you think of that?"

"Did they have high heels?"

Another roar of laughter.

"I told him to beat her with a stick but he was afraid of her."

Fearing the conversation was taking a turn that might upset Rathwan, I said I didn't think anyone should beat anyone. The old man was quiet for a while, then asked a question in a very serious tone.

"He asks if it's true you go back to England soon."

Yes, sadly it was true.

With richly worded Bedouin largesse, Rathwan's father invited me to return whenever I wanted. I was welcome any time. He hoped I would write to the family and not forget them. I must come back.

I said I very much wanted to return to Jordan.

"*Inshallah*," he said with deep sincerity. "*Inshallah*."

I felt I should attempt the elaborate politeness a Bedouin would bring to the situation. I thanked him, praised his hospitality and said if he or any of his family came to England I would make them very welcome; or if they were in England and needed help, I would be pleased to assist them in any way I could.

Father seemed to like this. He nodded, grunted and went off to talk sheep with the Syrian. Although I would have been in two minds if I found some members of the family on my doorstep, Umm Tahir for instance, I'd have welcomed Alia or little Yousef. But Yousef had firm ideas about England, as shrewd as they were innocent. Before I'd been offered Radya to buy, I'd told Rathwan I wanted to steal Yousef and take him home with me. Rathwan asked Yousef if he'd like to go to England; the little boy looked very startled.

"I wouldn't know how to speak to people. They wouldn't understand me. I'd be lost, have nowhere to live and I'd starve."

I thought about all the young people sleeping in London shop doorways who did speak the language. No code of hospitality saved you in London.

Rathwan's father offered to drive us to Amman on the day I had to fly home.

"If she misses her plane she will have to stay here and marry my friend. I don't think she'd be happy about that."

A friendly farewell handshake with Umm Tahir; a wave for the little ones, who were mostly more interested in a bout of rubbish-eating; a bit of a tearful hug for Alia and Yousef. Rathwan was putting my bags into the Toyota. I took a long last look at the desert. Father saw what I was doing.

"He asks if in the city where you live you have a house like my aunt's."

"A bit like it, but smaller."

A flat actually, no expanse of roof for sunning myself, another block of flats for a view.

Rathwan's father gazed out over the desert and sighed deeply. "To live in a house," he said, "is to live in a grave."

CHAPTER 5

Enemies

Rathwan telephoned every week – nothing interesting, nothing much to say in a five-minute call across money-eating miles. But the calls weren't for conversation, they were to remind each other we were out there.

"I think we know now this will work," he'd said, as I left him at the airport.

Once a month or so he wrote letters. They came on lined, floral-bordered notepaper, the sort an elderly maiden aunt might use. It was uncanny to think of him making his small printed characters on this dainty, fussy paper, his strong hands holding a pen too tight, his sun-beaten face concentrating, his big, mysterious eyes squinting slightly in the effort to write the language he spoke so determinedly well. The writing was care-fully centred on the small pages and the content formally structured like the letters a child is made to write as a class exercise. Up to a point. He'd begin with enquiries after my health, assurances of his wellbeing, mention of the unchanging weather, the presence or dearth of tourists . . . then he'd have a wild, affectionate outburst, a rebellious indulgence in 'forevers' and 'always'.

He telephoned the day after Valentine's Day, puzzled by his card from me, and listened unprotestingly to my self-pity over my empty letter-box. He was a Muslim; how could he know about the commercial exploitation of some second-rank Christian saint? Nevertheless, he was all apologies. A week later a feast of a card arrived, like something from a Victorian museum: embossed flowers, hearts, bits of lace, feathers, a treacly poem and his love. Who knows where he'd got it, what poor Christian stationer he'd hunted down and hounded round his shop until he produced a worthy card.

I was thrown straight into work on a television series on my return from Jordan; it was highly lucrative but in the hands of a producer who proved to be clinically insane. I wrote for the madwoman by day and read insatiably about the Middle East by night. Some weeks went by before I stopped feeling dazed and went back to my circle of friends to explain myself; it was hard to say what had happened between Rathwan and me. A few people – people I'd have expected to know better, people who'd be appalled to be described as racist – had an expression on their faces that mingled surprise, pity and concern as they said, "An Arab, Annie?" I never felt quite the same about them again. But true friends were all set to get out their Visa cards and go back to the Middle East with me.

I took the money from the television series and ran, intending to get back to Rathwan as fast as possible. But as soon as I'd bought my ticket to Jordan, the BBC offered me a job making a programme in East Africa: all expenses paid, my first, grown-up foreign assignment. There would be a turnaround time of only two days between Africa and Jordan; feeling like the absolute queen of intrepid adventure, I packed for both trips at the same time and told Rathwan I'd see him after I'd seen Tanzania.

In different circumstances, my feeling that I was a very glamorous creature indeed would only have increased when I found my flight out of Dar es Salaam was delayed, forcing me to lounge away the extra hours beside a swimming pool at the airline's expense. As it was, I passed the time chewing the sunbeds ragged and losing my mind as my turnaround margin narrowed down.

Thinking I might lose them, thinking I had all the time in the world, I'd left my Jordan documents on my mantelpiece at home. I dashed off the plane from Africa and rushed to my flat in central London and back, making the Jordan flight by ten minutes and forgetting to swap luggage. Instead of arriving in Amman a suntanned, elegant, important-type person, I was a maniac with hair on end, dirty clothes and wild, staring, sleep-deprived eyes. But Rathwan didn't notice; he was simply relieved that I'd arrived in one piece. He'd been worried not to find me safe at home re-organising myself when he'd telephoned the previous night.

"Something could have happened in Africa, a lion or something. You could have drowned," he said.

I assured him that the BBC took good care to insure its

correspondents against drowning by lions. Gibbering with tiredness, I had him dragged the length and breadth of my adventures in Tanzania before dinner was halfway through. I showed him the photographs I'd had developed during the long wait for my London flight. He flicked past an over-enthusiastic number of pictures of giant tortoises that I'd taken on an island off Zanzibar, thinking they were a wondrous sight.

"You didn't look at these. Look, they're as big as sheep."

He glanced at them, disapproving, unimpressed. "Yes. I don't like those things. I never liked them."

As if his life had been wall-to-wall trouble with giant tortoises.

A splendid lunatic struts the streets of Amman: tall and deliberate, he parades down the centre of the road with an umbrella that's all spokes, a tail coat and a carefully constructed wire-and-cardboard crown. Everyone has seen him; no one knows anything about him. Bashir and Salah had told me that he seemed to have been around the streets forever, a mobile local monument. Rathwan thought there was more to it – he suspected the man was English, his only evidence being that the man's occasional shouted ravings were peppered with English swearwords. Rathwan also felt the tail coat was a good starting point for making up a story about a member of the House of Lords fallen into scandal and hard times. The six-foot-tall, blue-eyed oddity in the crown certainly didn't look Jordanian. Inventing his biography amused us until we could ferret out the truth. He would be on our list of essential projects along with Gertrude Bell.

Rathwan was amazed to find me up and alert and checking on lunatics from my hotel window at eight o'clock the morning after I arrived from Africa; in fact I'd been up and observing since dawn.

The market street outside my window at the Hotel Wadi had worked itself up to an unbelievable din by eight o'clock – trucks, shouting, music, buses, occasional outbursts of rhythmic clapping and chanting from salesmen trying to drum up trade: "*Shebab, shebab, shebab, shebab*" (Come on, guys) – it sounded like the backing vocals on a 1950s song.

Peeping out between my curtains, I'd watched the crowd scene set itself up from nought to mania in a matter of an hour. First off the blocks were the men selling cold juices (known as sherbets); they had many more preparations to cram in than the men hawking socks, cigarettes, perfumes and second-hand clothes. The sherbet vendors had large plastic containers to wash and set up before the ice truck came, after which coffin-size slabs of ice were unloaded, broken up with chisels and hastily thrown into the containers. 'Juice' that seemed to be more colour than flavour was then added to the ice – bright orange, glowing yellow, and there was a liquorice one as lurid as a shade of black can be. A parade of sherbet acolytes turned up and the liquid was poured into the elaborately wrought brass pots carried by these street peddlers, who looked like something out of a bad Hollywood version of the Arabian Nights, wearing full Ottoman Empire costume including fez and curly-toed shoes. The brass pots were slung from heavily reinforced belts and clearly weighed a ton; some of the peddlers carried plastic cups stacked in loops on their belts, but those more sensitive to tradition than to hygiene carried a brass cup and a scrap of cloth to wipe it. Tied to the top of their pots they all had long feathers as luridly coloured as the juice inside; as the peddlers wandered around bus stations and other crowded areas, the bobbing feathers made it easy for the thirsty to spot them at a distance.

I watched as piles of old clothes were flopped down on trestle tables. Alongside were the new products of Syrian sweatshops – pink, fluffy children's jumpers emblazoned with hearts and the name 'Ben Elton' were heaped up on one table. Why a North London Jewish comedian had captured the imagination of Jordanian children I couldn't guess. I have a Japanese friend in London who fronts a band called the Frank Chickens; she said the name came from a Japanese brand of pencil, any use of English words, no matter how indiscriminate, being thought extremely hip in Japan. In the Syrian clothing industry, the Frank Chickens school of English sloganeering seemed to have caught on: I saw 'I am Torminater', 'Ratfighting', 'New Things Street', 'I am in Sun' and 'Nice Cornish' mysteriously decorating small chests.

A good deal of what was being sold beneath my hotel window was the product of a favourite Bedouin sideline: smuggling. The cheap children's clothes made by low-waged workers in Syria came in tax exempt; the brand-name perfume and cigarettes, which again usually entered the country via Syria, could have pitched up in Amman from a hijacking in Woolwich or Wisconsin.

As the trading day got started, waiters wearing grubby semblances of uniforms could be seen weaving their way through the crowd. On their heads they carried huge tin trays loaded with meals for workers, or hotel guests like Rathwan and me who would telephone orders through to this delivery service if we were feeling too lazy to cross the road to a restaurant. Our favourite breakfast came from only a hundred yards away, and consisted of bread and thick lentil soup. It sounds a revolting start to the day, especially in hot weather, but the delicious home-made broth set us up for hours and cost only pennies, including a tip for the waiter.

However, the morning after Africa we had to stir ourselves into the street with less lazy folk because the hotel lounge was heaving with enormous men in black track suits: bellowing, backslapping giants who scared the staff and sent a young Egyptian woman fleeing back to her room at the sight of them.

"They are a wrestling team from Hebron," Rathwan discovered. "They usually win."

Having first tracked down Salah and Bashir, we breakfasted at the cafe opposite the Roman theatre. We talked about the big news: Tujan Faisal, a feisty woman, had been recently elected to Jordan's parliament. Well, it was big news to me; Rathwan and his friends didn't think it quite so exciting but they politely offered up what information about her they knew – which was less than I'd already gleaned from reading the English-language papers.

Tujan Faisal was careful not to represent herself as a subversive hooligan. She made sure she was interviewed at home with her three children and constantly emphasised her role as a good

Muslim wife and mother; but she was talking tough about women's rights, particularly alterations to the laws relating to women's status and the inheritance of property.

The small group of Islamic Fundamentalists in the parliament had objected ferociously to her presence. For one thing, even shaking hands with a woman who was not a relative was against their beliefs; and as in parliaments everywhere, shaking hands while thinking poison was a staple activity in Jordan's assembly. The Fundamentalists also didn't like the way Tujan Faisal looked; a Circassian with long, unveiled blonde hair and Western clothes, she was considered a bad public example and a provocation. Not that she turned up for work in hot pants, but her chic business suits, with their skirts that reached to just below the knee, were still too much for the Fundamentalists.

A week after parliament had begun sitting, the newspaper cartoonists were still ridiculing Tujan Faisal. One cartoon depicted her grinning stupidly in a skimpy, cleavage-thrusting mini-dress while a Fundamentalist politician approached her with a pile of clothes saying, "Please, put on modest clothes and let us concentrate on the business of parliament." In another, the male parliamentarians were meeting in a traditional Bedouin tent while a veiled Tujan Faisal was off to one side kneading bread dough by a fire. "When she's made our lunch, we'll begin," one of the Islamic Fundamentalists was saying.

There were plenty more, none of them particularly funny. I'd noticed that Jordanian newspapers were packed with cartoons on a 'never mind the quality feel the width' basis. The images were crude and often cruel, although from this cartooning fever one or two clean lines of talent stood out: Hajaj, for instance, a young Palestinian who drew for one of the most conservative papers in the country, *Al Rai*. His political cartoons were more subtle than the run-of-the-mill stuff and I'd been told that his work was often turned down by his paper for being too radical; they nevertheless kept him permanently on the payroll, recognising they'd found a gifted if wayward soul. Not bad for someone entirely self-taught, whose first career had been as one of the dusty boys selling bread from a tray on Downtown streets.

Unfortunately for the standard of the cartoons about her, Hajaj had better things to do with his pen than get involved in the bitching about Tujan Faisal. His fellow-cartoonists, like most people in the country, found the Fundamentalists a little foolish; but the way they chose to portray a blatantly respectable woman as a silly floozy seemed to me a rather double-edged attack. Why not show Tujan Faisal as she was, all dignity and sobriety, rather than play along with the Fundamentalists' distorted vision of her? Perhaps Jordanian cartoonists had few opportunities to draw pendulous breasts and curvy thighs with impunity, and were gorging themselves on the chance.

King Hussein had come down heavily in support of Tujan Faisal and eventually the Fundamentalists glowered sulkily into silence. Subsequent events proved that they might have held their noise from the start: the election of Tujan Faisal didn't herald a rush of female politicians, nor did she fulfil her early promise as a champion of women's rights. She entered into the workaday grind of politics and after a few years grew tired of trying to move immovable forces, becoming much the same as one of the boys.

At the time of her election, however, there were high hopes. Bashir and Rathwan agreed that almost every woman in Jordan was behind Tujan Faisal. (Women over eighteen had had the vote since 1973.) And the men? Salah said something and laughed.

"The men," Rathwan translated, "know it is wise to say they like her. Especially if they are married."

Rathwan and company were more impressed by King Hussein's backing than interested in the woman herself: "If the king respects her then we support that."

For someone with such an otherwise lively mind, Rathwan could be stubbornly obtuse on the subject of King Hussein. That the king was irreproachable I'd learnt not to challenge, but when I asked Rathwan what would happen to Jordan when it lost its good, smart king he looked at me as if he'd severely overestimated my intelligence and would prefer never to see me again.

"His successor will take over. Both his brother and his son are ready for the day."

"But what if they're not as good as King Hussein?"

"He has taught them everything he knows. He has chosen them carefully."

Wisdom couldn't be taught, I maintained; one very special king couldn't set up a dynasty and guarantee that it would only get better.

"He is the king. He knows how to organise the future."

On and on against a brick wall. I abandoned the argument, as it was the first time I'd made Rathwan really angry. I didn't even throw down my royal trump card, King Talal, Hussein's father. Talal had reigned for a very short time before giving up the throne, ostensibly because of 'ill health'; the truth was he was barking mad. I'd think that would be a fairly unlucky DNA strand to have lurking in the system of a hereditary monarchy. Was King Hussein conducting long-term genetic tests on his family or just keeping his fingers crossed?

When we were in Amman, Rathwan and I could be perfectly happy just sitting around at the Roman theatre doing nothing. So, that afternoon, once we'd finished with important dull chores like taking my clothes to the laundry and mailing some postcards home so that no one else would suspect I'd been drowned by lions, we headed for the theatre. I sat up on the steps reading, and Rathwan sat by Ismat's house gossiping with other tourist guides. He even managed to make us some money when the urge took him, seizing on groups of tourists to guide round the delights of the Roman theatre.

Ismat's daughter was sick and he'd gone to the hospital leaving the guides in charge of his territory for a few hours. Inevitably, boys got in – but I had a lot more trouble with a little girl. Aged about seven, wearing jeans, a T-shirt and an expression on her face that would scare horses, she strode up to me, bullying away two little boys I'd been chatting to. She was accompanied by her sister – a tear-stained, nose-running toddler – and a brother aged around five with what looked like a fresh duelling scar down his face.

"*Kurdi*," said the little girl. Then she pointed to her brother and sister: "*Kurdi, Kurdi*."

I smiled and nodded. Kurds.

"*Kurdi*," she said again with a stamp of her foot.

I nodded and read my book. She bossed her siblings into sitting down beside me and stood herself on the step below me, hands on hips, trying to stare me into submission. If any other kids tried to muscle in on me, she gave some very tough talk and was soon rid of them. This battle stance had nothing to do with fondness for me or desire for a lock of my blonde hair; she held out her hand and said "Dinar, dinar" several times.

I ignored her. "*Kurdi*," she stressed again, as if this was something she'd learnt would tug effectively at heart strings. Mine were a bit too hot and tired to be tugged. Besides, the empty pockets I showed her were genuine: Rathwan was carrying all our money because he didn't lose it or get overcharged, and because he had a genuine horror of the way I'd stuff money in my pockets instead of folding it neatly in a wallet after carefully and repeatedly counting and straightening it. I don't know why the West has this notion that Arabs are profligate with money; Rathwan, like everyone I met in Jordan, was razor-sharp shrewd to the last penny.

Razor-sharp all round, the Kurdish girl wasn't believing my empty pockets for a minute. Muttering terrible curses, she stomped off to the gardens outside the theatre, dragging her brother and sister behind her like dolls. I saw them group round a woman in black who was carrying a baby – their mother presumably. The children pointed up at me; the woman shook her head and sent them back up towards me. Maybe she'd told her daughter to try harder. The child certainly did. She counted my silver rings – seven – and showed me her own empty hands. She had me turn out my pockets again. She got the little boy to sit on my knee while she pointed out the hideous scar on his face; I wondered if she'd inflicted the wound to improve his usefulness as a begging prop. When the toddler started to remove one of my rings, I decided the time for a counter-attack had come: "*Ruuh!*" (Go!) I shouted and planted the boy firmly on his feet. Little sister burst into tears, big sister glared at me with snarling contempt, spat at me and left me to stew in my selfishness.

I could've got money from Rathwan for her, I'm sure she did really need it. Poor Kurds, massacred and persecuted wherever they put themselves. I'm sure some of my best friends would be Kurds, if I'd ever met any apart from this ferocious little girl.

She might have wanted me for a best friend if she'd encountered the tourists Rathwan and I had a run-in with at Jerash a few days later. Two young Americans were making a shameful scene at the entrance to the town's Roman ruins, waving a copy of a guidebook and shouting.

"We write for this book and we'll write about this," one of them was claiming belligerently. "It's offensive to foreigners. We'll say that foreigners come here and just get insulted."

The young Arab behind the ticket desk, far less stupid than they were or than they thought he was, pointed out that their guidebook had only recently been published and that it seemed unlikely to him that it needed updating already.

This so riled one of the pompous brats that he demanded, "Who's in charge here? Who's the top man?"

The ticket-seller asked calmly, "Do you want the top man in Jerash or in Jordan?"

Rathwan and I sniggered, upping the Americans' pitch of rage. Their complaint was that at Jerash, as at many sites, Jordanians were charged a lower entrance fee than foreigners ('visitors' is the courteous term that's actually used); at Jerash, the difference amounted to little over a pound. The ticket-seller patiently reiterated that the difference in pricing was an official Jordanian policy, not something he personally had any control over.

The boys weren't having that. "Then you should tell them. You must tell them it's offensive to foreigners."

The ticket-seller assured the tourists that he would indeed tell 'them'. Confounded by this gentlemanly stalemate, the more ridiculous lead brat whispered an aside to his pal: "I'm going to say something really offensive now." And, as if it was really worth it over a couple of dinar, he said to the ticket-seller, who wore the black-and-white *kefiyah* of a Palestinian, "In Israel it's the same price for everybody."

In case he hadn't been stupid enough, he repeated it, louder. "I said, in Israel it's the same price for everybody."

This was so deliberately offensive – to the point of deserving a punch in the face – that the ticket-seller completely ignored it, as an adult overlooks a child's unwitting obscenities. He asked quietly if the boys wanted tickets or not.

"OK. Right," said the fuming idiot. "So when Jordanians come to America, we'll charge them double for everything."

Rathwan had an avuncular tone which he adopted when he was in his most dangerous mood.

"I have been to America many times," he lied, with a confident smile. "You *do* charge double for everything. Now if you don't want tickets, we would like some."

As the quieter American had already waned from support of his companion to mortification, he backed off immediately. The loud brat couldn't resist an infantile parting shot: "Go ahead then. If you've seen one crappy ruin in this country you've seen them all."

My guess was that in his own country he had relatives and acquaintances who were fervently hoping he would remain travelling, as far away and for as long as possible.

For days afterwards I thought of good retorts I could have come up with. I could at least have given the brats a short lecture on the justice of the pricing system. It cost the none-too-wealthy Jordanian government a small fortune to excavate all these ruins, employ staff, administrate sites and build rest houses for the benefit of visitors who could afford to fly across oceans to complain. It was perfectly reasonable that the people of the country, many of whom could barely afford the bus fare to the sites, should be charged an entrance fee within their means. In London I found it infuriating to pay taxes to help maintain the British royal family yet still be charged a huge entrance fee to see a fraction of Buckingham Palace; the Jordanian two-tier price system was a sign of a government that gave a toss about its people. And far from wanting to offend foreigners, the government carefully considered their needs as well. Tour guides like Rathwan were required to have a work permit, issued only after they'd passed exams in historical knowledge and foreign languages. Tourists were seldom bothered by freelance hustlers and were encouraged to report them; my persistent junior Kurd really was an exception. The American boys couldn't have seen much of the world if they couldn't see that Jordan was an unruffling place to visit. Oh yes, I should have told them . . . I should have said . . . Gertrude Bell would have taken a stick to them, bellowing in her fluent Arabic until she'd attracted an angry crowd to set upon the brats.

As it was I was useless in defence of, well, plain good manners at least. All I managed, in English, was: "Stupid boys. They don't write for that book."

The man, wearied and a little pink around the gills, said, "I know. What nationality are you?"

"Irish."

"That's different," he grunted as he handed us our tickets.

"He sees you are different anyway," Rathwan assured me. But I wasn't sure. What I really hadn't liked was the way the Americans had kept looking to me for complicity in their argument: another foreigner. But I felt I was more connected with the ticket-seller than with them; an insider. I suddenly wanted to speak fluent Arabic, to be able to truthfully say Rathwan was my husband and be 'us' rather than 'them'. To change sides, to blend into Jordan and be with Rathwan forever.

Not that he was asking. And the mood passed as soon as I got hot and bothered climbing around Jerash and some Bedouin women clucked at me for wearing shorts.

Hard luck on the Americans that they missed Jerash. Only a third of the spectacular Roman city had been excavated so far, and it seemed likely that some of it would remain forever buried unless archaeology won out over the living and the busy modern town built over acres of the Roman one was demolished and its inhabitants done away with.

Ancient Jerash was one of the star cities of the Decapolis. Its inhabitants could boast that they had two temples, two baths, two amphitheatres, a colonnaded forum, several triumphal arches and fertile land all around them. Earthquakes, beginning with an almighty one in 747 AD, brought down much of Jerash and it had been completely deserted by the twelfth century. It was gradually forgotten until a Circassian colony settled there in 1878.

Now hard work went on daily to put the remains back into upright order. Teams of labourers, usually Egyptians, were squatting everywhere sweating and chinking at stones – the restoration was being done with the same basic tools as the original building, except for one spoilsport with a cement mixer. If you shut your eyes the sound of an orchestra of tiny hammers against stone rang all over the city like the sound of goblins in a diamond mine.

A long colonnaded walk stretched far across the ruined city; Rathwan pointed out ruts in its paving slabs that were marks made by ancient chariot wheels. About halfway along, a flight of steps led to the temple of Artemis, patron goddess of the city. From the base of the steps, I couldn't see the temple at all; the steps had been arranged in flights of seven with a flat section between each flight to ensure that the long descent wasn't too dizzying. If you'd been able to make it right to the top, that is: there was a place of sacrifice before the summit, and only

163

citizens whose sacrifice was thought worthy of Artemis were allowed to proceed on to the temple; if not, they were deemed to have irritated the goddess and had to go back down until they'd mended their ways.

The larger of Jerash's two amphitheatres was far higher and broader than its counterpart in Amman. In the summer, a festival of arts and music was held here, with participants from all over the world. In less festive times, tour guides showed how the acoustics ensured you could speak in a whisper from one marked spot and be heard anywhere in the auditorium.

The second, smaller amphitheatre had cool, high-vaulted inner chambers and a terrifyingly steep rake. Undaunted, a group of schoolgirls in navy overdresses ran up and down the steps, shouting and taking photographs of each other. Another group in the same uniform sat at the highest point, singing and clapping. Until they spotted me. Then I had the pleasant experience of knowing what it's like to be a film star: I had to be photographed with every one of the girls, be repeatedly told how beautiful I was, sign autograph books, collect a hundred scraps of paper with scrawled names and addresses, and accept a dozen bouquets of hastily picked wild flowers.

"Write me, write me!" my fans begged. One told me she wished she was me: "I want to be an engineer but the family . . . I will not build a life. I will be married."

The glamour I held for them had nothing to do with me personally; it lay in their knowledge that Western girls did get to be engineers, to travel, to become writers. Did I have a flat? A car? Did I have a brother they could marry?

There was a cheer when I mentioned Tujan Faisal. "Very good. Very strong," said the girl who wouldn't get to be an engineer.

Rathwan tapped his watch after an hour of this. "Annie, their teacher is going crazy. She can't get them to leave for their bus."

I had to hide in one of the inner corridors of the theatre until they'd been chaperoned away.

Due south of Jerash, the Crusader fortress of Kerak had a large room laid out as a museum –a few unlabelled pots and unascribed stone lamps in half-empty glass cases, more dust than exhibits. The only item of real interest was a printed wall panel quoting our friend Gertrude Bell's description of her visit to the fortress. It had been a Turkish barracks in her day. She'd ignored the Turks and had 'a splendid picnic', something she tended to do when-ever she came upon a place of great historical significance. We'd already had our picnic that day – we wanted information. Rathwan found a tired-looking man in the museum's back office and asked if he could explain any of the half-hearted display.

"These things are found here from Crusader times. The Turks rebuilt but also destroyed many old things at Kerak. But we have only begun to excavate," he told us with a sigh.

In Jordan, 'we have only begun to excavate' could be a national slogan.

The curator invited us to have tea in his office, a fright of strip-lighting after the murk of the exhibition room. "The trouble with Jordan is we have so many ancient things – too many. Foreign archaeologists come and find wonderful ancient things.

'Look, you must preserve this, display these finds,' they say. But often they go home then and that's that. We are left with the things."

He discussed a site called Umm Rassas where Swiss archaeologists had uncovered two fantastic Byzantine mosaic floors. The Jordanian Department of Antiquities ordered them covered up again until the Swiss came back with the money to preserve and display them.

"And what is more," he sighed again, "there is a whole town at Umm Rassas, piled like rubbish, waiting to be excavated. This needs to be organised." He sighed again; I was beginning to catch terminal depression from him. "The thing is, there are living people who need the government's money more than these dead things. The dead things have always been here, they will remain here but the living are only living a short time."

We nodded sympathetically. But when we escaped from him, Rathwan didn't really agree:

"After all, the dead things are why tourists come. I am living and that's how I live – tourists."

The wide assortment of the dead is what blows the mind in Jordan: Edomites, Greeks, Seleucids, Moabites, Nabataeans, Omayyads, Ammonites, Romans, Mamluks . . . Anyone who had any sort of empire or run of military luck passed through and left their traces.

And sometimes, people from races I'd thought were no more than cracked exhibits in display cases these days turned up in the Hotel Wadi lounge to add to the mix of nationalities already inhabiting it.

One evening I found myself sitting next to a slightly drunken

Assyrian. A little old man from a race I'd imagined had died out with the Bible, last seen coming down like wolves on the fold. Now they were lambs, fleeing the wrath that Saddam Hussein visited upon anyone he thought might be looking at him sideways.

Although the phenomenally high rate of chronic alcoholism in Iraq wasn't confined to any one group, perhaps the old Assyrian had more reason than most to get drunk. Between the spring of 1987 and February 1988, the Iraqi government destroyed thirty-one Assyrian villages and twenty-five Assyrian monasteries and churches. The little whisky-scented man at the hotel, his daughter and son-in-law had fled the country, eventually meeting up with relatives in Jordan. He pronounced himself among the last of his people to make it out of Iraq. The Assyrians, he said, were scattered or done for.

The Assyrians were Christian, light-skinned, Amharic-speaking and closed tight within their own culture. In explaining their awful situation, the little man described Arab Iraqis as 'simple animals'. "Not thinking people. All Arabs are dirty people with the simple minds of animals." He ridiculed the Arab Iraqis for their delight in uniforms and medals, telling me that Saddam's military regime suited the Arabs fine because they loved shiny things and bright ribbons. "Simple animals."

He asked me to join his family for dinner the following night. Indicating Rathwan, who was sitting nearby reading a newspaper, I asked if my friend could come with me.

The Assyrian looked shocked. "That fellow?"

He regained his composure and smiled. "Of course. If he would like to come."

167

I relayed the invitation to Rathwan. He looked at the man, nodded and returned to his paper.

The following afternoon a note arrived cancelling the dinner due to 'unforeseen circumstances' – that I'd have an Arab in tow being what I suspect was unforeseen.

Arabs hadn't systematically eradicated my people. But I still couldn't bear the way the Assyrian had looked at Rathwan.

"I don't like these Assyrians," Rathwan admitted, when we talked over the incident. "They're dirty people who think they're better than everyone else." He agreed that they'd suffered – but he still couldn't like them.

I had a similar failure of altruism when we ran into a couple of Bosnian Muslim refugees.

Jordan had airlifted out a sizeable number of Bosnians and installed them in hostels. The pogrom against the Muslims of Bosnia was then at its height and Jordan, unlike England for instance, had decided that refugees were something its meagre economy just couldn't get enough of. Rathwan had bumped into this particular Bosnian couple when they first arrived and had shown them the sights to cheer them up. He'd bought them dinner and tried to amuse them as best he could, given that they spoke only fragments of Arabic and a few words of English.

The couple were in their early twenties and very European-looking. She had hair hennaed to a shade of aubergine, pale skin and dark, drapey, hippyish clothes; he was red-haired, freckled, wore jeans and a combat jacket, and was rather full of himself. We were passing the time of day at the Roman theatre when they appeared, delighted to find their pal Rathwan. At the sight of me, the Bosnian man instantly began nudging Rathwan and winking at him. Rathwan smiled weakly and tried to distract him with questions about their wellbeing. The man addressed all his remarks to Rathwan; the woman kept looking at my feet for some reason. I was wearing gym shoes, she wore high-heeled black sandals. Perhaps there were cultural shoe differences we could have discussed, but when I smiled at her she looked away to gaze adoringly on her man. He disdainfully asked Rathwan if I was a tourist. Rathwan told him no, I was a friend.

"Oh, *friend*," said the Bosnian, making an unmistakably sexual gesture. Rathwan looked like he'd been slapped in the face with a wet former-Yugoslavian flag.

"No," he said sharply. "A business friend."

The Bosnian laughed in a 'Yeah, sure' sort of way. Then, ignoring me completely, he asked Rathwan to go out with them for coffee. Rathwan declined, citing me as an excuse. With a look of contempt, swiftly followed by a suggestive wink at me, the man turned on his heel and his girlfriend trailed off after him.

"I'm sorry." Rathwan sat down with a sigh. "I didn't know what to do. They were nice before."

"Well, they're not nice now."

"He is very young."

"If I meet him again he won't live to be much older."

Rathwan laughed: "Jordan rescues the poor Bosnians but Annie destroys them."

The world is full of cultural generalisations formed on the basis of an individual encounter, or punctured by an individual encounter. I'd heard people say that the Iraqis' souls had become sick. In my reading and documentary-watching at home I'd found out so many terrible things that Iraqis had both done and had done to them – how could they have souls that were anything other than bitter, poisoned or wasting to insensibility?

Although every Middle Eastern nation seemed to send an ambassador to the Hotel Wadi lounge, Iraqis held the majority of the seats. I'd panicked at first when Rathwan told me the hotel was Iraqi-owned. Less than two years after the Gulf War, was an Iraqi hotel really the best place for me to stay?

He'd laughed: "Oh yes, I forgot that Saddam Hussein told all Iraqis the war was your fault."

It was good for me, having it spelt out for my slow brain that of course there were Iraqis who would no more hold me responsible for the actions of Western rulers, secret services and military leaders than they'd like to be blamed for Saddam Hussein. How could ordinary Iraqis stop what he did or made them do? My friends and I had marched to protest about the Gulf War; living in a democracy, we weren't arrested, tortured or killed. But we also didn't stop those in power over us doing exactly what they'd decided to do.

Encounters with Iraqis in Jordan, particularly in the early days, were a chastening lesson about the subtle effect of propaganda, even on those like me who imagined they were perceptive and unprejudiced. Finding myself face to face with real Iraqis in the Hotel Wadi lounge, fear and guilt made it difficult for me to look them in the eye. But they bought me tea, offered to share their food with me, gave me cigarettes and never once looked at me in a way that could be interpreted as anything more than curiosity or surprise at my unlikely presence.

The elderly owner of the hotel wasn't around the premises much himself, leaving the daily grind of the business to his loud, friendly son Mahmoud. About twenty-five years old, built like a Hebron wrestler, Mahmoud ran the place with a lot of shouting and much dependence on the calm efficiency of Omar. Mahmoud's trouble was that no one took him seriously. I would watch him scream at his employees for upwards of fifteen minutes, expecting them to be terrified; but they would just half-listen to him and go about their business unperturbed. They knew what I soon knew: Mahmoud's deafening bark was far worse than his bite. In fact, if he could possibly avoid it, Mahmoud would never bite, fire anyone or even get too tough about being paid. On several occasions, if Omar hadn't double-checked the figures, Mahmoud would have undercharged me.

"Han!" Mahmoud would shout up the stairs as I was packing. "Give me more money, Han! Sorry!"

And Omar would show me where Mahmoud had gone wildly wrong in calculating my bill.

Too many sad life stories: that would be my real complaint against the Iraqis. There was one old man, tall and thin with a face that could have doubled for John Gielgud, who haunted the foyer of the Hotel Wadi. Elegant of carriage and formally polite, he was often miles away in his stare of heartrending sadness. Rathwan befriended him and discovered that he had recently retired after almost a lifetime in the Iraqi army. He had a daughter who'd married a Kuwaiti and gone to live there several years prior to the war. Long after the Iraqi retreat from Kuwait, the old man still hadn't been able to make contact; he didn't know if his daughter and grandchildren had survived. Then, on a business trip to Jordan, he'd bumped into a Kuwaiti who lived in the same street as his daughter; she and her whole family were alive and as well as anyone could hope. A letter to her had gone back with the Kuwaiti. As direct contact between Iraq and Kuwait was impossible, her father had asked her to telephone him once a month at the Hotel Wadi. She did call, but connections were unreliable and it was impossible to ring at pre-arranged times; so he would barely move from the foyer, waiting in painful hope for her call.

Sometimes he met up again with the kind Kuwaiti stranger and sent parcels to his daughter; sometimes he received letters and photographs that she sent care of the hotel. Whenever I went back to Jordan, my trip coincided with one of the old man's visits. He liked Rathwan and was always happy to see us, his usual aloofness melting into kindly smiles and delight in Rathwan's chatter. We'd have long tea and cigarette sessions together, noticing a change every time we met up. His inner dignity and patrician grace didn't falter, but his circumstances were crumbling away.

He made frequent trips over the border. Quite apart from his personal mission, like all the better-off Iraqis he came into Jordan to buy groceries, medicines, clothes – almost everything was hard to get and prohibitively expensive in Iraq. There were heavy taxes to pay for to-ing and fro-ing across the border and the exchange rate on the Iraqi dinar was pitiful. The less well-off Iraqis crossed into Jordan to sit at the roadside selling anything they could. Younger Iraqi women sold themselves in such numbers that it was made illegal for Iraqi women to travel alone. Stories of brothers bringing their sisters into Jordan to work as prostitutes were tragically common, bringing desperate shame on the girls and their escorts alike. We sometimes saw beautiful young Iraqi girls in the company of old, unsightly foreign men; a marriage to a foreigner of any kind was a way out.

As the direct effects of the war over Kuwait receded, the plight of Iraqis got worse. At first our old gentleman had arrived in his own Mercedes wearing crisp new Arab clothes or a good suit. But his suit was a little shabbier each time I saw him, his eyes wearier; on our last meeting he was wearing labourer's clothes and an old anorak. He looked exhausted.

For the first time he accepted a cigarette from me rather than insisting I smoke his. We bought him tea and then Rathwan made our excuses, saying we had an appointment.

"What appointment?" I asked as he hurried me out.

"He will feel he has to buy us tea now. I don't want this."

Our old man was all but ruined. "He told me he arrived in his car but it's not true. Last time I know he came in another man's car. This time he came hitchhiking in a truck with the other very poor Iraqis. He will sleep in the truck. He is only in the hotel for his phone call."

I almost burst into tears.

"I know," said Rathwan. "I feel like this for him."

"Perhaps his daughter . . . ?" I suggested.

"Do you think he would tell her?" Rathwan was right.

The Western sanctions were destroying Iraqis: good, bad and victims of the accident of their birthplace. Saddam Hussein sometimes held back supplies to worsen the effect of the sanctions and to allow him to blame the rotting despair of his people's lives on the West. The sanctions and Saddam Hussein were both killing our old gentleman – and neither side gave a toss about him, his daughter or the phone calls he could no longer afford to receive.

Our last sad meeting with him took place in September 1995. By the spring of the following year, no one at the hotel had seen him for months.

In Jordan I often felt I was being pitched into a sea of news headlines and would swim to the surface a more broadminded person. The trouble with news headlines is that they're what come shrieking to form your opinion when you're in a tight spot, while the quieter, broader parts of your mind are still grinding into action. When an Arab leaps out of nowhere at a popular tourist site and starts firing off a gun, your first thought is, "Ah yes, here's a crazed Islamic Fundamentalist come to shoot foreigners." Having met the sort of foreigner a Fundamentalist might have in mind – our American charmers at Jerash for instance – I could see that we didn't always help ourselves; but being shot dead seemed an extreme lesson in etiquette.

One afternoon, I was sitting at my usual post in the Roman theatre, up in the high seats on the sunny side, reading. Rathwan kept to the shade by Ismat's house, sometimes dozing off, more often talking to friends. I had bananas, a glass of tea and the peace of mind that comes only to those who know what it's like to look round and see no sign of a fearsome Kurdish girl child.

Absorbed in my book, I thought I heard gunfire but decided it was a car backfiring – why would there be gunfire? Then three things happened at once. I saw the tourists opposite me run from their seats to hide in an archway, I heard Rathwan shout my name, I heard a gunshot. I looked up to my left and there was a young Arab at the very top of the theatre brandishing an automatic pistol. If he was there to shoot tourists, there was now only one in his line of fire.

I was a long way from the archway on my side; moving towards it, with all his attention on me, seemed like an extremely bad idea. I slowly curled up as small as I could, wondering how much it would hurt before I died. If he couldn't hit my head, maybe . . .

I heard another shot. A shout. Bashir was stalking up the steps below me, his gun at the ready. The gunman trained his weapon on Bashir, who was moving across and away from me now; I held my breath, not wanting to do anything that might distract the man into shooting me instead of Bashir. (He was a policeman, it was his job to get shot.) I could see the other tourists, huddled in the archway, looking terrified for me, signalling me to move – but I couldn't see a safe spot I could reach without panicking the gunman.

He didn't shoot again. He ran right along the top of the theatre – he'd soon be facing me – I had only a moment. I slid down the steps and threw myself flat behind a low wall at the section perimeter. I lay there watching my hands shake, waiting to hear more gunfire. But there were only shouts. And then Rathwan was beside me, smiling, urging me to come out. I stood up, laughing a little too much, a little too high pitched. Bashir and the gunman had vanished. The tourists were fleeing out of the gates – a trifle churlish of them not to check up on me, I thought, considering they'd almost had the sight of me being splattered in a hail of bullets to liven up their holiday anecdotes.

Hammad, a normally sour and unfriendly tourist guide, betrayed a whole other side of himself, clasping my hand and laughing the way I was, hysterical with relief.

"Are you all right? You must feel terrible. Sit down, sit here," he fussed at me.

"*Alhamdilillah*," Ismat said, close to tears. "She's still with us! *Alhamdilillah*."

Rathwan was more interested in finding out what had happened to the gunman than thanking God for my deliverance. He charged out of the theatre when some lads shouted, "They've got him!"

I was flabbergasted. Hammad solicitously persuaded me that it wouldn't be wise to follow Rathwan. He and I sat chain-smoking, recovering ourselves, while Ismat, humming tautly, stared transfixed at the spot where the gunman had been.

When Rathwan came back he was very excited. "They've caught the bastard!"

I could have shot him.

Some Johnny-come-latelys rushed in to see what all the excitement was about. Bashir returned to a good deal of backslapping. He lit a cigarette and told us he'd been doing all his brave stalking with only one bullet in his gun, after firing off his first bullet to scare the stalkee right at the beginning. On his way off duty, Bashir had forgotten to empty his old service revolver – just as well. He showed me that his hand was shaking and laughed. "If he fired, my head would have split like one egg, Annie."

"You were very brave."

"No. I wasn't thinking. I was halfway up the steps and then I think about my fiancée but it was too late."

I'd thought about her too somewhere in all my fear, thought about the buckets of money he'd laid out for a wedding he wouldn't get to attend. We all had more cigarettes and simmered ourselves down; except Rathwan, who was watching from the gate for more news. Salah, pouring with sweat, rifle in hand, came in with the latest update. Our gunman had been caught and the police had given him a good thumping in the van; for scaring them more than anything else, I suspected. He wasn't a crazed Islamic Fundamentalist at all: he was a drunken wedding guest. It's a Bedouin custom for male wedding guests to ride around the deserts firing celebratory rounds into the air – fine in the wide open spaces but not in the middle of rush-hour Amman after a few drinks. The gunman had fired a shot through the sun-roof of his car, scaring pedestrians, then scared himself by firing on the police when they flagged him down. He'd been chased up the back of the Roman theatre, which is where I came into the story.

"You know how it is in cowboy films when the Red Indians drink alcohol?" Hammad said to me. "It is like that with some Muslims."

We sat around drinking tea and reliving the adventure for the next couple of hours. Bashir's captain turned up and took him back over his movements. Up at the top of the theatre, they found an empty nine-millimetre magazine. The man's gun had been empty for most of the time I'd thought I was going to die.

Bashir had it brought home to him how lucky he'd been, because the automatic fire couldn't possibly have missed him from that range, no matter how drunk the gunman. There were a great many assurances from Bashir, Salah and their captain that I wasn't to be frightened, wasn't to think this was usual in Jordan. All the same I began to feel that Jordan wasn't so safe – it was a place where at any moment something awful could happen.

I wanted Rathwan to take me back to the Hotel Wadi.

"Good idea," Hammad said. "She's had a shock." Amazing, this solicitousness from a man who usually thought it a kindness if he even bothered to sneer at me.

Bashir and Salah offered themselves as an escort, but I suddenly didn't want to be near any more men with guns.

"I'd like just us to go," I muttered to Rathwan.

He did as I wanted, but I could feel his regret at having to tear himself away from his friends, who'd begun re-telling the story yet again.

"What's wrong?"

Like slamming automatic gunfire, I told him why I hated him.

"You didn't care if I was all right – you didn't do anything. I could have been shot."

"What could I do? I don't have a gun."

"I'm not talking about that. I'm talking about afterwards."

But I *was* talking about that. I don't know what I'd wanted – Rathwan to snatch Bashir's gun and run at the man himself, to race up the steps and fling himself on top of me? The idea that he'd cowered hiding with Ismat and Hammad disappointed me so much.

"The man was afraid of the police not of you. Why would he shoot you?"

I told him what I'd thought when I saw the gunman, the news reports about Egypt and Algeria where rebels had gunned down foreigners to make their point to the wider world. I had thought this must be personal.

Such a thought hadn't crossed Rathwan's mind. And he'd been angry with me for not moving. I told him my excellent reasons for staying put – although in the telling, I wondered how much I was simply justifying it to myself and if what I'd really done was act like a rabbit in car headlights. Rolled up like a hedgehog before the wheels of an oncoming juggernaut: so scared there's nothing to do but wait.

Anyway, never mind what I'd done or not done. I was the one being shot at. He was the one who was completely insensitive.

"Hammad was kinder to me than you. You don't care at all."

"I knew you were OK."

"I wasn't. I'm not."

Actually, I was by then – except about him.

He went quiet for a while. "You are right. When I saw you weren't hurt I was more interested to see what was happening."

"Admitting it doesn't make it better."

"No?"

"Go away."

I left him at the entrance to the hotel looking ready to die.

I counted my money: just enough for the hotel and a bus to the airport. If I didn't eat the whole of the next day. Furious to be so dependent on Rathwan, I decided I'd rather starve. I resolved not to let being shot at put me off my stride – I'd get on with my life.

In the morning I went out to get an interview with Tujan Faisal; I'd concentrate on my career, now my heart was stunned cold.

I walked to the Ministry of Information, where a friendly official made some phone calls for me. While I waited, I ate all the biscuits I was served with tea. There was one meal anyway.

Tujan Faisal's answer was no. Not until the following week, not even for the BBC. She'd had so many interviews and so many hassles – she wanted a clear week to settle into the job.

Rathwan had been to the hotel looking for me. Left a note begging me to meet him at the Roman theatre, promising to keep checking the hotel for me. I sat in my room drinking the last of my mineral water. I'd be flying home the next day – was I really going to leave things like this? I'd make us both miserable because I wanted heroics? Because I wanted a huge demonstration of sympathy over an incident that had already receded to being an interesting anecdote rather than lurching trauma? I wanted him unthinkingly heroic and wanted him thinking and considerate. How reasonable. What if he expected a whole lot of perfection out of me, then where would I be?

As I walked up to the Roman theatre I could see Rathwan standing outside, talking intensely with his father. I thought he hadn't seen me, as he didn't wave or do anything to acknowledge me; closer in, I realised from the expression on their faces that something was very wrong. Ismat beckoned me through the theatre gates. Rathwan and his father remained locked in their fevered but low-voiced discussion as I walked past.

"Please," Ismat said, ushering me into his house. Father's irritating friend was there, the ankle-ogler who'd thought I was to be had for a few camels; he was cheery and full of talk of wanting to take me back to his *bayt*. Ismat made tea, agitated and exchanging looks with me that told me he knew the stupidity of the remarks he was being asked to translate. Then he refused the project altogether:

"I say no speaking English. Is right?"

"Right," I smiled. However, Father's friend continued to make warm eyes at me. I wanted to leave and find out what was happening with Rathwan, but Ismat said, "You wait here!" in a tone usually reserved for small boys.

Rathwan's father appeared at the open window, a face like thunder. He beckoned his pal out and didn't acknowledge me at all. In a few moments Rathwan came in – pain like weight on him.

Ismat busied himself washing tea utensils. Rathwan took my hand.

"Are you all right?" he asked.

"Yes, don't worry about me. What's happened?"

His father had turned up unexpectedly and asked Rathwan to

181

lend him some money. Not for himself, for his idiot friend. When Rathwan told him he was just about broke, his father refused to believe him and turned nasty. He swore at him and said: "If you don't give me money I don't want to see your face again."

Rathwan promised him he really was hard up but this wasn't good enough for Father.

"My father isn't how he should be with me. He never helps or advises me. Always he takes from me or tries to destroy me."

I recognised this. I knew about this kind of father.

Ismat was shocked and couldn't hold back a comment any longer: "A father must not speak to a son this way."

Rathwan nodded. "My father and his friend have plenty of money. If they need cash they have all their animals to sell."

I suggested that his father might have been boasting to his friend – my son works in the city, he's loaded, time he did me a favour . . .

"This is what my family think," Rathwan agreed. "They think I work with tourists, I must be rich."

Of course his father was furious when Rathwan refused; all his big talk turned to bullshit. But Rathwan felt there was a much deeper reason for his father's anger: asking for the loan was a test, an attempt to make Rathwan do something purely as an exercise in obedience.

"He doesn't respect my way of life. That's why he does this to me here, in front of my friends and colleagues," Rathwan sighed jaggedly.

Ismat was tormented by the injustice. "It is wrong," he said. "Rathwan very good. Good."

Rathwan asked me to sit with him in the theatre for a while, ashamed, I think, of showing so much emotion in front of another man.

"Thank you," I said to Ismat as we went outside, and I shook his little hand – because he looked so hurt for Rathwan, what I really wanted to do was give him a big hug.

"Rathwan love for you," he said as he closed his door. "Speak him."

There were seats in curved niches along the front wall of the theatre. Sitting on one of them hid us from any friends who might show up – for once Rathwan wouldn't want to see them.

"I don't know what to do," he said, heart-weary. "I can't forget so much. My mother, sick for a long time. Ever since we were children he hasn't been right with us, didn't look after us or give us money for school things. Even now he tries to stop the children going to school so they can work with the sheep and goats. I was with my mother in the city for a long time and he has never been right with me."

Later I read somewhere that a father's curse is the worst thing that can happen to a Muslim son. But it wasn't this cultural spin on the situation I saw when we sat picking over Rathwan's pain that day. I was seeing him completely, not as someone exotic or mysterious, something always 'other' – he was my friend with a scar in his psyche that I recognised all too well. How had we found each other? Deep underneath speech and details, the same.

It wasn't just his past that was hard. "When you're not here," he told me, "I stay out with my friends until I'm ready to sleep. But usually I don't sleep well in my room."

I realised that for all his popularity and affability Rathwan was often lonely. I thought of the tiny spartan apartment he'd described to me, with its one mattress and two boxes of possessions. To live alone like that was a torment for a Bedouin. He was lost between two worlds: trying to find independence in the city but not yet ready to leave the pull of Bedouin family life and the close communities of the desert.

There was me. But I was leaving the next day.

"I don't know what to do," he repeated, on the verge of tears. "No matter how old I get, my father can always destroy me."

I tried telling him the answer wasn't to let his father wreck his peace of mind, because that was exactly what he intended to do. Rathwan agreed; but I knew myself that knowing the answer and feeling it were a long journey apart.

"Think," I told him. "Think how much you've already achieved in spite of everything. You've done well, been strong and survived. Your father hasn't destroyed you and he won't. He's only hurting the surface of you, not who you really are."

"Thanks be to God," he said.

"Thanks to who you are too. You won't get destroyed by him."

He smiled. "If only you were here every day."

The surface of him was himself again.

He got to his feet. "I really didn't lie to my father. I have two dinar. We need more for a good dinner and a taxi to the airport."

"We can go by bus."

"Buses. I hate those things, I've never liked them."

He went to sit with Hammad to watch out for tourists. The guides had a system of taking turns to show people round – they didn't compete, they were a team. But Hammad could be an unreliable player. He might say he hadn't had a turn when he had, he might catch tourists just outside the gate and pretend he'd met them somewhere else. Hammad had lost everything in his home town of Jericho in 1967; it had made him loathe anyone who wasn't an Arab, and even then . . . It was said that he set people against each other, that he always tried to get others into trouble – but he'd been good to me and apparently he gave up several turns that day so Rathwan could make a few dinar and leave early.

When Rathwan caught a large group of German tourists and went round the theatre with them, I went back to sun myself. As a sort of therapy I picked the same seat I'd been in when the shooting happened. When Ismat saw this he jumped to his feet and applauded me.

"Actually, I would like to return to this question of you being shot," Rathwan said over our good dinner. He'd remained fairly subdued all day, brooding on the quarrel with his father.

"It's not important now."

"I let you down. I acted like a teenager. Believe me, if I could turn time back I would have taken better care of you."

"I know."

"It's terrible that you're leaving now. Too many things have happened at the last minute. I need you here to talk to. Who can I talk to when you're away?"

"There's Bashir, Salah . . ."

"Annie, they're my friends, but . . . For instance, this business of my father. Why do you understand my feelings as if you are inside me?"

But I was leaving the next day.

CHAPTER 6

Football and Other Games

The four grizzled old Iraqis watching television at the Hotel Wadi merely pouted a little at the jingoism of the US opening ceremony for the World Cup. The Saudi Arabian was noncommittal to begin with but looked like he was going to choke to death when Diana Ross started prancing about the screen in a skimpy silk vest with her nipples standing out like wheel nuts while she sang "I'm coming out." She certainly was. The poor man looked round the lounge, desperate to find someone to share his outrage, but the Iraqis remained calm, bored even. Then a nightmare display of well-rounded dancing girls in shorts poured onto the screen to traumatise the Saudi still further. And far from him finding an ally in the lounge, I was sitting there, showing my ankles, smoking cigarettes, and being allowed to stay up late watching football with the men. Not just watching, but voicing loud support for Bolivia, shamelessly and repeatedly having opinions. By the time the second injured Bolivian was carried off on a stretcher by hefty American girls, the Saudi took to his bed before he fainted and needed a stretcher himself.

When he'd gone, there was a strange flurry of talk about Maradona and Argentina from the Iraqis. One of them made a remark that the others found hilarious. I asked Rathwan what was so funny.

"It's a joke. This man said that two Kuwaitis committed suicide when Argentina lost the World Cup."

A joke? I accused him of missing the punchline and possibly the set-up as well.

"No, that is all. An Iraqi joke."

We wondered if the Hotel Wadi's recent face-lift had been an Iraqi joke. The walls were all newly whitewashed in a normal sort of way, but curlicues and whirls of multi-coloured neon lights blazed from the lounge ceiling and what appeared to be an Astro-turf carpet – but could have been the fake grass greengrocers use for displays – had been laid in all the public areas.

Rathwan was bored by football; he absolutely failed to understand the emotion the roaring Iraqis and I invested in it. Bearing in mind that Iraqis can approach vocal haemorrhage over the price of groceries, the rows over football were sky-sundering in force and volume.

"What's wrong with you all?" Rathwan complained incredulously, as we screamed over the rapid demise of Bolivia. "Bolivia? Do you have family in Bolivia? Do these Iraqis know any Bolivians? Do you?"

When Ireland played Italy the next night I at least had my nationality to claim as mitigation for my yelling mania. The

Iraqis began by backing Italy and I thought we might fall out – but they gradually switched sides, not out of any deference to me but as Ireland started to run rings round the Italians. Rathwan protested by making fun of us: with his nose buried in his newspaper he would let out indiscriminate cries of "Offside!" or "The ref's blind!", greatly amusing himself. (He did this in Arabic and English – the unimaginative language of the football fan is universal.)

Ireland won, and Iraqis claiming Irish ancestors and best friends congratulated me as if I'd scored the winning goal myself. Rathwan suggested I'd be well advised not to take off my shirt and roll on the ground like my countrymen on the screen.

He asked if he could possibly have the rest of the evening off. Magnanimous in triumph, I agreed and we went in search of Bashir and Salah but found Faraj instead. I hadn't met anyone Rathwan liked who I didn't, but Faraj . . .

When I'd first come across him I'd found him irritating, but figuring that he would only be a very minor character in our lives I didn't give him much thought. Rathwan had so many friends and hangers-on. Faraj counted among the hangers-on who asked Rathwan for favours. He found them hard to refuse because Rathwan liked to help people who were old, sick or vulnerable in some way that worried him. Like Eid, for instance, a beautiful little boy with green eyes, a smile like sunshine and a serious chance of growing up to look like James Dean. I'd accused Rathwan of bone idleness when I noticed that every time he wanted a newspaper or a cold drink, he'd send Eid off to the shops for him.

"I give Eid tips for this. If I go myself Eid will have nothing. My bones are not idle, this is how the system is."

Rathwan had started out as an Eid, hanging round the tourist guides after school, hoping for an errand to make money much needed at home. I noticed he took time to teach Eid English words, to explain things to him. Being an Eid was how Rathwan had got to thinking tourist guides were just the coolest guys in Amman, and bright, smiling Eid had obviously got to thinking the same.

I understood Rathwan's endearing protection of Eid, but although Faraj was poor and often sick I couldn't find any sympathy for him in my cynical heart. Faraj was probably in his late twenties: skinny, shuffling, with eyes set too wide apart in a head that was too small for his body. He would fuss at Rathwan till he got what he wanted, which was usually money. This time he told Rathwan that he was worried about his sister. She had been ill, she was married to a horrible man who was also ill, she lived in the far north of the country and Faraj couldn't afford to visit her. Rathwan immediately decided the far north would make an interesting expedition for all of us.

His lack of tact was one of the things that irritated me about Faraj. Having secured our financial backing for his trip, he insisted on joining us for coffee and went on hanging around until the last dregs had been drained from the evening; he even returned to the Hotel Wadi with us for still more coffee. Granted, Bashir and Salah spent quite a lot of time with us – but they were fun, didn't scrounge and knew to leave us alone occasionally. It was impossible to get rid of Faraj: when I said I was exhausted and went off to my room, Faraj just waved vaguely in my direction and carried right on talking to Rathwan as if I was the one who was peripheral to the evening.

But it was July and very hot; the prospect of escaping from Amman, even in the company of Faraj, seemed a good idea. I would miss only a couple of football matches.

Faraj's sister lived in Ramtha, a town up by the Syrian border. The whole area was a notorious hive of smugglers and Ramtha was the home of the queen bees. King bees. Tough bees at any rate: there were more heavily armed civilian men sauntering the byways than in South Central LA.

There was some sort of rumpus from small boys as we got off the bus. I heard Rathwan tell them I was an Arab. I didn't understand exactly what they were shouting but I heard the word *kaffiri*, which tends not to bode well. Nor did I like the corner-of-my-eye glimpse of them picking up handfuls of gravel.

Ramtha felt like it should have been a sleepy country town, but as well as the over-armed citizens there were a disconcerting number of new Mercedes and huge, two-storey, turreted and balconied houses. Despite recently increased border patrols, Ramtha's illicit trade in cigarettes, alcohol, cheap clothes and other goodies from Syria was flaunting itself in far too many brazen flashes of wealth.

Not everyone was a rich buccaneer with treasures aglint in the sunshine. Faraj's sister, Basma, lived in a small, paint-peeling house by a patch of waste ground and wasn't doing so well at all. Yet she obviously wasn't reduced to such desperate straits that she was pleased to see Faraj: she greeted him with an indifference verging on resignation. However, her face lit up in warm welcome of us two strangers.

A plump woman who moved with a stiff-legged limp, Basma was lucky not to have got her looks from the same ugly-bag as Faraj; she had huge, gorgeous eyes, flawless dark skin and a regal bone structure to a head she held high. With vivacious pleasantries, she tried to hide her embarrassment at being caught unawares by visitors. She discreetly sent her many children scuttling to household tasks and continued talking to us while flapping a damp cloth at anything that might be dust or flies, and throwing cushions and mattresses around the living room to make it more comfortable.

We met the horrible husband, Shaban, over tea. He was in a wheelchair and almost immediately asked me how he could get help to obtain medical treatment in Britain. Rathwan gallantly put that one over the crossbar by assuring him that medical services in the UK were not what they used to be, in fact we'd hardly a hospital left.

Shaban's back was done in somehow and he had a shattered, grossly swollen knee that I hoped he wouldn't display again too close to lunch. He'd been a truck driver to and from Iraq until he'd been in an accident which killed three people and maimed him. Hearing of an accident on the roads to Iraq didn't in the least surprise me; those Iraqi driving games were for high stakes. Basma and Shaban had seven children and they didn't know if he'd recover sufficiently to ever drive again or be able to find some new line of work – barely literate, he wasn't in with much chance of a desk job.

Basma suggested we might like to see the surrounding countryside while she prepared lunch. Faraj complained that it was
far too hot to go traipsing about. Basma looked at him wearily
and reminded him that there was a neighbour, five minutes away,
who'd recently bought a taxi. He could take us on a sightseeing
trip without Faraj having to unduly exert himself.

The taxi was parked beside two gleaming Mercedes in the
runway-width drive of a palatial but unfinished house; breeze
blocks were piled round the sides and black plastic covered
un-topped turrets. Even before it was completed this was the
biggest building in town. Was it the lair of the chief smuggler?
Was the taxi a front? Of course. It plied its trade in all apparent
innocence while strapped under the chassis were . . .

"They are from Kuwait." Faraj brought me back to earth.
"They're Jordanians who used to live in Kuwait. They came back
last year."

Harith, the head of the family, came out to greet us and invited
us into his mansion, where we were served Pepsi and cubes of
watermelon on cocktail sticks. Originally from Ramtha, Harith
had lived in Kuwait for thirty years. He had imported Mercedes,
a lucrative line in pre-war Kuwait; his son and grandchildren had
been born there. The taxi was the son's attempt to make a fresh
start while they tried to set up a new import deal in Jordan.

"But Jordan cannot afford many more Mercedes than it has
already. Perhaps we will find something else."

The family hadn't left Kuwait entirely empty-handed, judging
by the further evidence of the contents of the enormous room –
half a dozen pastel-print sofas, smoked-glass coffee tables, gold

finish on everything that could possibly be gold finished. A mixture of Arabic and European knick-knacks filled three glass-fronted teak-veneer bookcases: brass camels alongside horse brasses, that kind of thing. There was a vast television, a huge stereo and what might have been a polar ice-cap but was probably a crystal chandelier. Nothing quite matched: quantity had been heaped up in the room as a more satisfying buttress against disaster than quality.

Harith had grey hair, inaccurately streaked with Grecian 2000, and a manner that shifted between a car-dealer's shrewdness and utter bewilderment. He certainly hadn't expected a foreign visitor in Ramtha but the diversion from regrouping his life seemed to please him. Harith only spoke a little English, but we staggered through a list of famous Jordanian sights I'd seen and a sketch of my origins. Just as I was bursting to ask him about Kuwait but felt it wouldn't be tactful, I was certain he desperately wanted to ask me what on earth I was doing hooked up with two Bedouin boys in the middle of nowhere.

The Bedouin boys were plainly uncomfortable. Faraj was embarrassingly awed and price-asking about the more impressive objects in the room. Rathwan, perched on the edge of a pink sofa, was dignified, courteous but eager to escape; he was neither impressed by nor at ease with conspicuous consumption. And Faraj's carry-on was enough to make the cat blush.

Khalid, the taxi-driving son, was fat and babyish-looking. He had several fat children, who were more entitled to look babyish but perhaps not to look like pampered little bullies in their brand-new Western clothes, all patent leather shoes and ruffles.

One of them always seemed to be hitting another one, and all of them were constantly shovelling fistfuls of sweets into their chubby jowls.

Although his children hadn't inherited them, Khalid had gentle good manners; he chatted to me in English while attempting to separate a squabbling pair of his offspring. Rathwan looked at him, peeved.

"Your English is good, Khalid. Where did you learn it?"

"Just in school."

"Oh?" Rathwan said, as if he were a particularly vindictive spycatcher general. "It's very good for just school English."

Rathwan did this sometimes: puffed out his chest at men he thought were impressing me. It wasn't a crushing possessiveness; I ignored him if he started. He would get himself into unnecessary sulks, misreading my curiosity about people. If I was naively open to other men's friendliness, it was only because I felt I had the safety of a retreat to Rathwan to protect me. Khalid turned out to be sweet, and very lonely out here in the no-man's-land and rural hooliganism of Ramtha; there were no sinister motives to his friendly chat, I'm sure. But Rathwan watched him closely every time he spoke to me in his English that was, to my ears, no more than senior-school standard.

To keep my distance, Rathwan took the front seat in the taxi. Khalid drove us out into the wilds, where the flex and fold of the remote hills became more and more beautiful. Rathwan relaxed, excited to see what was to be seen in this part of the country he didn't know.

Khalid parked up a cart track by a tree-lined stream, promising us that we would soon see 'elegances'. It was cooling to be around so much foliage. We walked to find the 'elegances', intrigued by a distant sound of splashing and gleeful shrieks. Khalid told me his wife was away, staying with her grandmother in Amman for a while, depressed by the turbulent uprooting of her life in Kuwait. "Like me, she is Kuwaiti born."

Shortly after the Iraqi invasion, the family had escaped through Saudi Arabia. Khalid seemed apologetic about their exodus, implying he'd have stuck out the dangers if it hadn't been for his wife and children. It was unlikely they'd be allowed to go back. The migrant labour required to run Kuwait would never again be supplied by Palestinians, Egyptians or Jordanians if the Kuwaitis could help it; after the Gulf War, they looked to India, Pakistan and East Asia for the help they needed with everything, from running hospitals and businesses to cleaning the streets. The money no longer sent home by workers in Kuwait left a big hole in the economies of the out-of-favour countries, but their governments' attitude to Kuwait in the war hadn't gone unnoticed.

No one had ever liked Kuwait very much: too rich, oligarchic, denying official status to people who might have lived there for generations but were originally from 'outside'. If Saddam Hussein had been a nicer person he might have won a lot of support in the Arab world for invading Kuwait; as it was, he won a good deal in spite of himself. When the American troops arrived in Saudi Arabia, forty thousand Jordanians signed up at the Iraqi Embassy to fight for Saddam. Although the thin hopes of dispossessed Palestinians looking for a hero lay behind many of those statistics, the Jordanians had always had more in common with Iraq than with Kuwait. Every country has a race it makes 'Polish' jokes about: for Jordan and Iraq the butt had always been the Kuwaitis – even their accent was mimicked as ludicrous and archaic. King Hussein's official neutrality during the war was only a veneer over the delight most of his people took in the come-uppance of Kuwait. Much vicious revenge had been taken on the despised Kuwaitis that they wouldn't forgive or forget in a hurry. Many people like Khalid, more Kuwaiti than anything else, were exiled to their original homelands, confused, still grasping a little of their wealth but stripped of everything else that had gone to make up their sense of identity.

We came to a rocky escarpment where a natural spring flowed through a graceful olive grove: a definite 'elegance'. We traced the spring back to where it bubbled up from caves higher up in the rocks. It had been split into two courses – one went to water crops in the fields below and the other to fill a natural pool where some young lads were yelping and splashing. Khalid said that the pool was about ten feet deep, but as it was only as wide as a lanky lad's arm-span and a couple of leg-lengths long, there was a good deal more plunging than swimming going on. For a spectacular leap into the water, some of the boys swung off the overhanging boughs of an ancient fig tree. They were all bare-chested but wearing long trousers; one was plunging with a baseball cap firmly plastered to his head. They didn't seem overly concerned that I was watching them but they did ask Rathwan if there were more tourists coming; if I was to be followed by a coach party of foreign females, the plungers might have had to look to their modesty or kick up a fuss at the invasion of their secret.

In the blazing July sun, it was a great strain not to jump in fully clothed and join them. But my escorts moved on before I had a chance to make a sodden show of myself.

Our walk took us up to the hilltops overlooking Syria. Traces of abandoned terrace farming gave the golden slopes a dizzying aspect: miles of faint, descending ridges spinning out of sight against a sharp blue sky. Nearer to us, the land was rich and colourful: there were tiny, whitewashed farms set in vineyards and groves of apricots, and an improbable clutch of Friesian cows clustered under some fig trees. Just behind them were two small fields of pale blue opium poppies – hardly enough to merit alarmist talk of another sideline for the smugglers of Ramtha, but then I don't know how much opium you need to start a business. The fields looked small enough to be for the farmer's personal use; perhaps the hallucinatory strangeness of the black-and-white cows among the figs was a scene he'd set up for himself to gape over while out of his mind.

"Just elegant, isn't it?" Khalid said and I realised where I'd heard this before: Marilyn Monroe exclaimed it over and over in *The Seven Year Itch*. Possibly Khalid had gleaned his English from more surprising sources than just the schoolroom.

"Just elegant," I agreed, trying to take in the foreground and background in a single glance: the prettiest of southern Italy backdropped by a scene painter of biblical epics.

When Khalid dropped us back in Ramtha, Faraj grandly asked how much 'we' owed him. Khalid's influences switched from

Marilyn to Anthony Perkins, looking as if he'd like to stab Faraj repeatedly with or without a shower curtain handy. I had a few sharp edges trained on Faraj myself, considering he undoubtedly wouldn't be in the 'we' who had to part with money.

"I didn't take you as a taxi, I took you as guests," Khalid said to me, almost turning his back on Faraj. Rathwan stepped in, thanking Khalid for his kindness and wishing him luck with his business. Faraj mortified everyone again by offering to pay for petrol. Khalid refused politely, teeth clenching. Then we all just stared aghast at Faraj as he laughed wildly and said: "Please, take some money. We are not Iraqis, we don't want to take petrol from people without paying."

Khalid shook Rathwan's hand, said it had been lovely to meet us and walked away without affronting himself with another look at Faraj.

Basma had run mad in our absence, doing up her sparsely furnished little house with whatever she had available: paper flowers in a plastic pot now flourished on top of the television, curtains had been put up at the barred windows, a poster of Jerash had appeared on the living room wall. Everything had been cleaned: all the concrete floors were damp, the bathroom was awash with disinfectant, and the scrub-faced children were in fresh clothes. Basma had changed into an embroidered light blue dress and made herself up exquisitely. Her husband remained as unsightly as before.

Basma gave us Pepsis and wondered if we'd like to rest a while as it was still too hot to eat. Rathwan didn't need asking twice and was soon asleep in the living room. Faraj wheeled

Shaban away to visit a neighbour. I hoped the neighbour was hospitable so they'd enjoy their visit for some time.

I shared a broken-down sofa outside the house with Basma and most of her children. Although we had very little language in common, we managed to communicate as we sat sunning ourselves. That she had married beneath her would be an understatement of the position this refined woman found herself in; nothing about her matched her setting. I noticed her unwitting flinch of repulsion every time her husband spoke to her. Then there was her struggle to rise above a poverty that was bound to get worse. With me, she seized a brief chance to think beyond Ramtha. She plied me with questions – what countries had I been to? what were they like? where would I like to go next? When I asked where she would like to go, she smiled ruefully and held out her hands to embrace the whole world: "Go," she said, with a deep sigh. Anywhere.

Meanwhile, we were all in Ramtha and starving. The sun was going down, Faraj was wheeling Shaban home, but Rathwan was still asleep. Basma hushed one of her daughters who started a complaint of hunger; but then she asked if I was hungry, and a shout of support went up from the children at my emphatic "Yes!"

"But Rathwan . . ." a child sighed.

"Rathwan!" I said scathingly and mimed dashing the water from a pail by the door in his face.

The children laughed; Basma looked more shocked than amused – hardly treatment she'd like for a guest in her home.

Before the last resort of water, the children and I pretended we were forced to make a vast amount of noise searching for my camera in the living room.

"Hush! No noise! No noise, remember!" I bellowed.

"Really, you should be shot," Rathwan muttered, opening one eye. He agreed to stay awake when I told him that small children were starving because of him.

The meal was generous; probably way beyond Basma's straitened circumstances. Salads, chicken, eggs, humus, felafel, couscous . . . Squatting around on the floor of the living room, we took a long leisurely time over eating, while Basma glowed in our appreciation.

But the atmosphere didn't add to my enjoyment of the good food. When she thought no one was looking, I would catch Basma giving a glare of pure hatred at her husband. In public she graciously played the role of thick-skinned good sport, even when Shaban asked Rathwan why he hadn't brought foreign girls for Faraj and him as well.

Basma tried to make light of this rudeness with a laughing remark to Rathwan and me: "Look at him – he is broken and still he chases girls."

Shaban went on to tell us that he had another wife in Iraq; he was considering bringing her over to share this house. I said he was mad to have another wife when Basma was so beautiful. He continued to insist on my opinion, in front of Basma and her feelings, as to the wisdom of installing the Iraqi wife.

"It would be disgusting," I said angrily.

Rathwan, who was translating, said, "I have told him your opinion more calmly."

Basma smiled at me; she knew my reply hadn't been calm.

This was the only private home in Jordan where I'd ever been offered alcohol; while Shaban boasted about the variety of liquor he had available, Basma shot him one of her looks of hatred. The conversation between Shaban and Faraj was coarser than anything I'd come across in a family home; actually, it was coarser than the talk in the Hotel Wadi lounge or in Ismat's house when it was packed to its low roof with soldiers and policemen. As a foreign girl I knew I was open to being treated without respect, but the crude carry-on in front of Basma was staggeringly insensitive. And Faraj was Basma's brother – he should have been livid; instead, he only added to the insults, making big talk to Shaban about how I'd be bringing my sister out to Jordan for him on my next visit.

"I'll do nothing of the kind!" I growled, ready to bite some heads off.

"Yes," Rathwan said. "I think their talk is too stupid for me to translate any more. I'll tell them that as well."

If it hadn't been for a silent communication with Basma, her eyes pleading with me to stay, I'd have insisted we didn't spend the night. The house felt so wrong and so miserable. It got worse too.

While we were on our third glass of tea, Shaban searched under a cushion and brought out a gun. He checked it, tucked it into his belt and re-positioned his wheelchair at the window so that he had a clear view of the road up to the house. He tensed every time headlights appeared, loosening when they passed; Basma and the children seemed not to notice this unsettling parlour game. I asked Rathwan to find out what was going on:

was there a smugglers' war about to break out or were we expecting the rent man? No. It turned out that Shaban had been to blame for the road accident. The family of the three people killed, instead of going through the customary process of accepting protracted apologies after protracted mediation by the local sheikh, had demanded forty thousand dinar in compensation. That was an impossible sum for a truck driver to find, as they probably knew – what they really wanted was revenge.

Perhaps the retaliation was to be directed at Shaban personally; hence Basma's apparent lack of concern. Perhaps there was a peak time for retaliation, because after two hours of headlight-watching Shaban merely locked the doors and windows and suggested it was time to sleep.

Rathwan and Faraj were to sleep in the living room with Shaban, but there was some confusion about what the form was with me. Rathwan told me that I could sleep on a mattress near him if I wanted, the household being a little careless of convention not to mention downright scary. But I knew that wasn't right. I picked up the mattress I'd been allocated and followed Basma out to the entrance hall, where she slept on an iron bedstead with the children on the floor around her.

Reassuringly, I saw Basma sneak a machete under her pillow before double-checking the front door and settling herself. I lay awake, waiting for a petrol bomb through a window every time I heard a vehicle, or a rain of machine-gun bullets to hammer against the house if a leaf stirred outside. How handy was Basma with a machete if push came to shove? If retaliators stormed in, would they massacre everyone or just the immediate family?

I woke up hot and bothered but apparently not killed by retaliators. Basma sat in the morning sun with me, drinking tea. She took note when Rathwan handed me my shoes; somehow they'd got tangled up in his belongings.

"Good," she said of him.

I nodded.

"Arab men," she tapped my pale arm, "like."

I touched her brown forearm: "English men like."

Basma smiled and pointed to Khalid's taxi driving past on the main street. "Me go England." She smiled again but it faded into a longing, tearful gaze into the distance. "No," she sighed. "No."

I felt weepy and grasped her hand. It wasn't fair.

Just before we left, Rathwan the Good handed me fifty dinar.

"Can you give it to Basma? It isn't right from me. You see how things are with her. Say it's for the children or she will be embarrassed."

I waited until her husband and children weren't around. Basma was more than embarrassed; she moved her hand away from the money like it had stung her.

"No. It is not for this."

"I know, I know," I said, and we looked closely at each other: Basma willing me not to think for a moment that she'd hoped for this payment, me willing her to know I didn't feel it was expected or necessary.

"*Atfal*," I said. Children. With a gesture of resignation, she accepted the money. Again, we both nearly cried.

"What's wrong, Annie, what's wrong? Not speaking."

I was going to kill Faraj right there at the bus stop. Rathwan motioned him away from me.

"You are sad."

"Yes, I'm sad. Basma . . . I expect I'll never see her again."

"And you like her. I see that."

"You like my sister?" Faraj butted in. "My sister very nice. You like Ramtha?"

I hated Ramtha and its gun-toting men. I hated Faraj, who obviously didn't give a damn about his sister; he'd just seen an opportunity for a bit of a jaunt at our expense.

On the bus back to Amman, in no mood to talk, I read Gertrude Bell while Rathwan, just for a change, fell asleep. Faraj, Rathwan's loyal friend, started telling me how pretty I was and how much he would like to visit me in England.

"Perhaps when Rathwan comes to see me," I said, with the last scrapings of tolerance I had for him.

"No. Just you and me . . ."

"Shut up! Fuck off!" I snarled, and banged the spine of my book down hard on his knuckles. He cringed away from me, sulking and afraid of the sudden looks from other passengers.

I felt I couldn't tell Rathwan about this sleazy exchange; not that I wouldn't like to see him punch Faraj in the throat, but the big softie part of Rathwan would have been so disappointed by Faraj's betrayal it wouldn't have been Faraj who was hurt.

Rathwan had been wasting so much sympathy on this back-stabbing creep. In attempting to explain it to me he had told me the background to their association, how when they had first met Faraj was out of work and ill, begging errand money in order to eat. Rathwan had bought him food and clothes, even found him a job as a cleaner at an army camp near Kerak. But I no longer cared if Faraj was the most tragic person in the entire universe, I wanted him out of our lives forever – gone. No more dogging our footsteps with his hangdog demeanour hoping for treats. He'd got me to reckon with now; I wasn't like Rathwan, I wasn't a nice, kind-hearted person.

The minute we got to Amman I announced that I felt violently ill; I think I even clutched my stomach in an agonised way. I kept whispering to Rathwan as I held pitifully onto his arm, terrifying Faraj. All I was saying was I wanted to go back to the hotel immediately before I fainted, but I panicked Faraj into leaving our company in a hurry, muttering something about getting back to Kerak in time for work.

Rathwan was surprised by my rapid recovery from what had appeared to be a sudden onset of the Black Death.

"I just wanted to get rid of Faraj. He makes me sick."

Rathwan smiled in the way he did when he was actually displeased. "You are very hard on him."

"Am I? All he does is take from you and embarrass you."

"I know," he conceded sadly. "He is trouble always. In my thoughts he makes me crazy but I feel sorry for him with my heart."

"If I see him again I'll go mad."

"Don't worry. He's gone back to Kerak. You know, he likes you, he thinks you are a very nice person."

Argh!

In case Faraj decided to throw in his job and scrounge off us for the rest of his miserable life, I hired a car the next day and hurried Rathwan out of town again.

"Where are we going?"

"Anywhere, you decide."

"Wadi Seer," he decided. "You will like it."

I hoped so – I was sacrificing several football matches for this jaunt.

It was skin-meltingly hot; after a sweaty half-hour on the road, we hit such a prolonged traffic snarl-up I had to pull into a restaurant for a cold drink or smash the hire car into a truck just to take the edge off my temper.

The restaurant was full of men, all staring at us. On my way to the Ladies I was shoved aside by a gang of them coming out of the Gents.

"Excuse me," I snapped at them, as they flattened me against the wall; they laughed at me as if it were my fault. The stare-athon continued when I came out again. I was hot, I was sick of being treated like a piece of meat by Faraj, by complete strangers . . .

Rathwan was drinking a glass of water. He looked very deep in thought.

"I ordered a Coke for you. Is that all right?"

I nodded, feeling the room's eyes on us.

"You look lovely. I didn't see this shirt before."

Every cell of me was so irritable that I could do no more than grunt. Rathwan smiled, but his reflective mood persisted. He told me that his relations with his father had improved. At least they were speaking to each other now.

"Except my father wants me to marry. This is the latest

pressure. He keeps telling me I am thirty-two and that I should marry." He paused – I was barely listening to him and he was searching painfully for the right words. "Of course it's you I really want to marry. I want you to live here with me always."

"Live here? You must be fucking joking!" I said and glared at one of the men who'd laughed at me. I was too absorbed in hating everyone in the restaurant to notice that the look in Rathwan's eyes had shifted.

"My problem," he said vaguely, pleasantly, "my problem is I love you – or I would throw this glass of water in your face."

I was as shocked as if he'd thrown it.

The men at the next table leered at me while they slurped and dribbled their soup – they were men, entitled to eat in any repulsive way they pleased and still smirk with an air of superiority at a mere foreign girl.

Rathwan apologised immediately for threatening me with the glass of water.

"No, I'm sorry," I said, as he drank down his armoury. "This place just gets on my nerves, all these men, all the hassle."

He frowned. "Don't say any more, Annie, or I'll think you've always hated your time here." He rubbed at his face, hot and tired. "The thing is, I can't go on this way, just these short visits."

"But us getting married . . . It's too soon."

"Soon? What is soon? Do you love me?"

"I don't know."

"Ah," he said. "Then that is different."

Wadi Seer was a good place to clear our jangled heads. The valley was green and restful; the traffic was far away, only the sound of goat bells on a nearby hill, birdsong and the occasional distant cries of children. Olive groves spread out around a small, seldom-visited castle and streams burbled through clumps of trees.

We'd been very quiet on the last stretch of the journey to this oasis, both thinking hard but neither ready to be the first to risk the subject of our future again.

Rathwan showed me the two lions carved on either side of the castle, the Qasr al-Abd, Palace of the Servant. It seemed rather grand for servants' quarters but there was no real explanation for the name. The building was said to have been constructed by the Tobiad family, governors of the region in the second century BC. The family were also believed to have carved out the caves in the nearby cliffs to use as stables. Locals still used the caves to shelter their animals in winter. Strangely, the caves were called Araq al-Amir: Caves of the Prince. Rathwan thought that some-time in the course of twenty-odd centuries, the original names had been mixed up: Palace of the Prince and Caves of the Servant was a more logical living arrangement.

The soothing greens and the hush of the valley gradually made me forget why I'd taken against Jordan. We had a picnic of ice cream and cashew nuts, watching the hillside opposite where a man worked his way down a zig-zagging track on a ridiculously overladen donkey. On another hill, two men were putting up telegraph poles along a path to a small house; it seemed like a very amateur job, done with a Laurel and Hardy excess of slipping, toppling and near-fatal accidents. On the road to Wadi

Seer, we'd seen a truck dragging one of these poles behind it; suddenly, the dragged end of the pole burst into flames from the friction. The men holding the safe end of it in the back of the truck stared at the fire unperturbed as it ate through their pole, as if they were conducting a scientific experiment and this was exactly what they'd intended to happen.

When he could see I was contented, might possibly listen to him without impatient interruption, Rathwan took the chance of talking to me again, to try explaining how he felt.

"It's the situation. I'm not very religious but it is to do with my religion. No, not just that. It is what our relationship expresses. At the moment it expresses that I have no respect for you. But you are not just some foreign girl to sleep with. I should respect you."

We watched the man with the donkey start to weave back up the hill he'd just taken so long to come down, and we both laughed spontaneously.

"You'll go away again and I'll think about you all the time. I'll remember the donkey man and the pole on fire and laugh when I'm alone at night. I'll remember lots of things and laugh. But I can't say, 'Annie do you remember . . .' because you're miles away."

"It's the same for me."

"I can't think of anything I want except you. And every time I see you I feel bad because I'm treating you like . . . This creeping around in hotels, this fear we will be caught – you deserve better. But if, as you say, you don't love me . . ."

My problem wasn't him. I knew him, there wasn't a bad bone

in him. The problem was Jordan – the Jordan he inhabited, where wealth couldn't cocoon us from tradition. Where I couldn't show my arms and legs, where even a wedding ring wouldn't stop me being something to harass. Only a veil might do that. The survival of his culture, his Bedouin tradition that I found so romantic, was the trouble ever-lurking in the background. It wasn't the small irritations, like the dress code and not being allowed to sit in the same room as him; it was knowing he'd be despised for taking a foreign wife and shut off from most of his family and some of his friends. Marrying me would not be the way to impress his father and regain his rightful position in the family. How long would it be before he resented that?

"It's too difficult for me here," was all I said.

"Is it your work? Can't you work here?"

There was the fax, the modem . . . But the work I'd been so disillusioned with when I first met him was branching off into new and more satisfying directions; it was a priority equal to my relationship with him. I had ambitions, a home, a culture of my own to keep up with and friends who couldn't pop round regularly to Jordan for a chat; I had another life, a parallel universe. How long would it be before I resented being lost in his?

"If you were my wife for even one year then I'd be happy. I'd have seen more of you."

"A wife for a year?"

"It's just a thought. If you couldn't live here forever. Or what about if you tried to come out for longer each time?"

"I can't afford it."

"No. Nor can I," he sighed.

I realised it wasn't all down to me.

"What about if you came to London?"

He smiled ruefully. "What would I do there – clean the streets?"

"Not necessarily."

But everything about him was in Jordan: his friends, his work, his identity. What did being a Bedouin mean to London? Where was the desert to escape to when he needed to calm down? How he'd hate living in a place where he wasn't the one who knew everyone and knew all the angles.

"I have been in Europe. I know how Arabs are seen there. When I travelled with the army, I thought we were looked on very badly. I could visit England but I couldn't live there."

"It looks like we're a bit stuck."

"If we could find something for both. Some way to rotate."

But international rotating takes money. It was a dubious future for two people with uncertain incomes.

"But I think we should marry first and then worry about the rest. At least then the sin and secrecy is over and no one has a right to look at us in a bad way."

I hated them. All of them. I wouldn't make a decision to please them. I couldn't make a decision. I searched for sidetracks.

"What about my gold? My big pink dress?"

He laughed. "If you want gold I can get you gold. But, you know, a marriage can be a very simple ceremony in the court."

"That's all?"

"Very easy. From that point, we can find a way round our

problems. From that point on, when we've made the commitment."

The course of true love would run a great deal smoother if it were easier to tell what it was. I didn't know if I loved him. I didn't know if I trusted him not to change. All the pressure of his religion and culture would be working on him; already, it had made him feel ill at ease about having an affair with me. Had he felt uneasy right from the beginning? What other changes might there be? In his attitude to my independence, for instance. All those stories in the newspapers, on television . . .

"Rathwan, I need time to think."

"Yes," he said sadly. "I was afraid of this. But you do mean you'll think, not just . . . You're not just saying it?"

"No." No, I wasn't just saying it.

"OK. Let's talk about something else. I hate this subject now."

Our donkey man had disappeared over the crest of a hill; there was just us and the birds. Until a crowd of kids descended on our peace and began playing football in the gravel beside the palace, shouting "Brazil! Brazil!" – they all seemed to be Brazil and to have several goals.

A tag-along toddler of indeterminate sex watched them for a while, then sat down next to us, saying "Hello!" repeatedly in English. Rathwan had a brief conversation with it and roared with laughter.

He'd asked, "Are you a girl or a boy?"

It had replied indignantly, "No. I am a child."

"No. I am a child." I laughed when I remembered it, alone at night in London. And I wanted to say, "Rathwan, do you remember . . ."

In several of his letters he asked if I'd made up my mind what to do about us. I always ignored the question. I needed more time.

Although Rathwan's English was near-fluent, he did have the occasional phrase that went askew. For instance, he'd always say 'lose your time' instead of 'waste your time'. I'd always liked that. Wasted time implies something that shouldn't need to but can be replaced. But time is lost, forever.

Rathwan had far more sense of wingéd chariots and the clock ticking away than I had. If I'd listened to him properly I might have heard what he heard.

CHAPTER 7

In Two Places

The astounding thing about Petra is its presumption. Little people saw great, sky-scaling mountains and thought, "We'll carve out palaces for ourselves the size of those mountains – it's the least we deserve."

The colours they uncovered as they began to carve out the sandstone must have convinced them they were blessed. Nature had made it easy for them to create one of the wonders of the world. Swirls of red, ochre, cream and violet; the inner walls had an accidental beauty a modern decorator would take months to copy in layered paint finishes.

The carvers were the Nabataeans, a nomadic tribe from Western Arabia. They didn't just hack out enough space for themselves to live in, didn't simply creep into their caves, grateful for the shelter: they made cathedrals for themselves. They went deep into the rock so the temperature in the caves bore no relation to the climate outside and they carved their

ceilings far above themselves, as if expecting their next generation to grow into giants. They took themselves up to the highest
parts of the mountains to create places of worship to their gods,
who lived at the top of the world. They brought their trade
caravans and the spoils of their raiding expeditions back to this
temple to themselves, and shut the world out.

For all their presumption, the Nabataeans' glory days ended
and Petra was forgotten. It became a legend, a lost city, an
Atlantis; until in 1812, a lone European explorer, Johann Ludwig
Burckhardt, disguised himself as a Bedouin while travelling the
hostile territory and found his way through the long narrow rock
cutting that led to the city. If had a moment in his life to top the
instant he stepped out into the light and saw the towering red
monuments of Petra, he must've had some life.

Petra had only been lost to Europeans, not to the Bedouin;
they'd lived there for centuries, irreverently but jealously guarding the gigantic ruins. While assuring enquirers that the place
didn't exist, they'd been clambering around the edifices, herding
winter flocks into the temples and staining the coloured interiors
with the smoke of camp fires. But in the mid-1980s the Bedouin
of Petra, a tribe called the Bdoul who are believed to be the direct
descendants of the Nabataeans, had to leave – all those stains
and goat tracks were wearing away the wonder for archaeologists and tourists. King Hussein had the Bdoul moved to new
villages to the north of Petra, but they crept back. Some very old
families had grazing rights, and a handful had the right to sleep
over with their flocks; but the mountains seemed to have a crowd
more Bedouin in them than the regulations permitted. Small

children skittered about high cliff faces, women herding black goats strayed every byway, young lads leapt around every corner trying to hustle a living.

No, not every byway, not every corner: it was possible to climb off on your own in Petra's mountains and believe there was nothing on earth but you and desolate rocks. But the lower slopes were a pandemonium of men and beasts. As well as herdsmen with mundane sheep and goats, there were men offering camel rides and boys with horses for hire. Horseback was the best way to arrive in the city, and hundreds of the animals stamped and steamed by the gates every morning: no plodding seaside donkeys these, but sinewy, temperamentally prancing Arab ponies. Sometimes they were hired out by old men, but predominantly by Bedouin teenagers who seemed to have been auditioned for their looks as much as for their riding ability. These boys had a distinctive style of dressing – their thick, checked shirts, jeans and red-and-white *kefiyah* made a composite macho vision as they galloped to work down the slopes from their villages. The Marlboro Boys, I heard a tourist christen them as we watched them preen around, cigarettes in the corner of their mouths, barely noticing the wild plunging of their horses; these Middle Eastern incarnations of the Wild West talked men's talk while waiting to do their dull work with foreign greenhorns. They should have been charging through stampeding cattle, galloping down on a bullion-loaded steam train, escaping the cavalry; instead they escorted us lumpen tourists through the Siq, the winding cleft in the mountains that led to Petra.

Harrison Ford had galloped through the Siq in the Indiana

Jones film. My dream was to do the same, but meandering pedestrians, the crowd of other horses and the regulations themselves forbade more than a seaside-donkey amble. The horses must have seen the film and known better: they kept trying to bolt, or to throw their cumbersome riders. The Marlboro Boys kept the animals just this side of control but managed less well with their bored expressions: transporting tourists was an undignified interruption to racing across hillsides and posing on mountain tops, which was what they were really put on earth to do.

If a tourist showed any sign of being able to ride a horse, the boys took more interest: they might be able to persuade the foreigner to break all the rules and cut their journey short by going at a gallop. I was easily persuaded. Charging through the Siq was exhilarating verging on the terrifying; Harrison Ford must have had a stunt man. I tried to keep calm as we swerved and swung about violently, narrowly missing collisions with sheer cliff faces, other horses, pedestrians . . . I reminded myself that the Marlboro Boys couldn't get a tip if they killed you, and told myself that the one perched behind me was really in total control of the horse and had probably been riding since he was born. Suddenly, we were ordered to cut to a walk by an older Bedouin man, who pointed furiously at the dust storm we'd created around coughing pedestrians in our wake; he noted down the identification number on our horse's bridle. Expertly bringing the animal to an abrupt standstill, my equestrian hero fell off headlong into the dust. He'd looked much older than his seventeen years until I saw the splintered pride when he picked himself up; we trudged the rest of the way in silence, passing other uncrumpled Marlboro Boys urging their passengers on. "You like to go faster? Gallop is much better."

When I first visited Petra, some horrible schemes for alleviating the increasing tourist traffic were under discussion: cable cars, cutesy little railways . . . disaster. And of course the horse-rental posse would be disbanded; pedestrians only through the Siq.

Rumours about the Marlboro Boys' behaviour were doing nothing to help their prospect of future employment. But I knew exactly how the rumours got started. My Australian army pal and I had an English couple join our group in Petra. Quiet, thinking themselves a little too intelligent for the rest of us, they were irritatingly dogmatic vegetarians who remained deathly pale throughout the trip, with much superior talk about skin cancer while the rest of us basked in the sun. They wore dull, dark clothes that accentuated their pallor and their determination not to have anything as silly as fun.

In their usual superior way, they went off exploring on their own one day and returned with him fuming and her ashen, even for her. Janet and John, as I'll call the couple, told us with martyred expressions that their holiday was ruined and they'd have to leave Petra immediately. At that moment our guide came over to see how many of us wanted horses booked for the next morning. Janet said, palely, that she felt she should warn everyone of her terrible experience that afternoon: her horse boy had groped her when she was dismounting.

"Maybe he was just trying to help," someone suggested.

"It was very deliberate," snapped our angry martyr, then resumed her near-fainting pose with John clutching loyally at her elbow.

I was chillingly reminded of *A Passage to India*: their trauma wasn't a reaction to whatever had happened but to the idea of foreign hands laid on her milky English dignity.

"Should've just kicked him in the nuts," my Australian friend said. Exactly.

If they weren't too busy arranging their appearance or gaining a bad reputation, the Marlboro Boys might have a surge of enthusiasm for their job and point out the two-thousand-year-old terracotta water pipes running along the high rock walls of the Siq. Originally completely hidden from view, the pipes were vital to the survival of the Nabataeans. They'd baffle their enemies by retreating down the darkness of the Siq after carrying out their raids and hide out for months. It was only when the Romans discovered their secret water channels that the Nabataeans were finally defeated, thirsted out under siege.

The Romans probably found Petra conveniently familiar: the Nabataeans tended to lift good ideas they'd spotted in other places, and their city included a Roman-style amphitheatre and a colonnaded street. All the Romans had to do was replace the Nabataean temple gods with their own.

Dushara, the Nabataeans' chief male god, was symbolised by a block of stone or an obelisk: he was too powerful to be represented by human arts. Similar block-represented pre-Islamic gods had their holy places in the desert of Saudi Arabia, where Mecca now stands; Mohammed appropriated their ancient sacred site for his new religion and upheld the belief that no human hand can draw the face of God.

Al-Deir, or the Monastery as it has been known since early Christian times, was originally a temple to Dushara. The scale of the surrounding mountains made it hard to appreciate how vast the monastery was, but when I was standing right at the foot of it I found the only way to see the top was to lean backwards in a slapstick, clown-about-to-fall-over sort of way. The most disconcerting thing about the monuments of Petra was the way they shifted dimension: some pillars were only carved relief protruding from flat surfaces, while others were fully rounded – it was as if the immense buildings were in the process of emerging from the rock faces and had frozen half-formed.

The lower part of the Monastery's facade was carved relief, but the upper sections were fully separated from the mountain behind. After climbing to the rock platform at the top, I was surprised to find I could walk right round it and gaze down a wide abyss between the platform and the mountain. The stone urn in the middle of the platform was, predictably, gigantic seen close to. The local boys who were sitting on the urn, dangling their feet in my eyeline, must have had prehensile tails tucked into their clothes to have got themselves up there. They were shouting greetings to the tourists far below on the ground and sharing a cigarette. A couple of them grew bored with this and possibly life in general, as they started a new game of leaping from the platform to the mountain – a mere skip of six or seven feet across the abyss. As I left them to it, more boys joined in, all daring each other into making the death-defying jump.

They stopped when they had attracted enough gasping spectators below and demanded money for the next performance.

"It would be a hell of a thing to get a picture of," one observer said.

"It would be a hell of a thing to be the one who paid a boy who fell," said someone more sensible. Not me – I was just watching with a cold feeling in the pit of my stomach as a tiny boy flew through the air, hundreds of feet above the ground, and . . . landed safely.

Behind the dizzying proportions of the Monastery was an even more dizzying view centred on Jebel Haroun (Mount Hor); this was traditionally known as the burial place of Moses's brother Aaron, and was marked with a small white dome. Aaron, or Haroun, is a particularly respected figure in Islam. Rathwan told me it was a difficult seven-hour climb to the top of Jebel Haroun and guides (himself in particular) discouraged tourists from attempting it – partly because there were easier places to take them, but more importantly because the mountain was considered a powerfully sacred place. The legend was that this was the only mountain in the region that didn't quake and crack open as being unworthy to hold the body of Haroun.

No longer so sacred was the High Place of Sacrifice, where the Nabataeans held the ceremonies of their religion. There is no real evidence but plenty of rumouring that they performed human sacrifices. The remote altar seemed suspiciously large, with its channels for blood to drain away; just looking at it sent my imagination into an overload of horror-film re-runs.

With Rathwan claiming some sort of climb-preventing terminal disease, and forgetting how unnerving the place could be, I set out one fine afternoon to find the high altar on my own. The weather changed and clouds darkened the sun. I lost my way, feeling a chill come over my insides that was nothing to do with the weather. When I finally reached the altar, a creepy wind shivered through the yellowing, dying patches of scrub among the rock . It didn't even seem like I was on earth any more. I was sure I was going to see some terrible, non-human horror . . .

"What a perfect place for a performance of *Elijah!*" exclaimed a beaming, elderly Englishman who suddenly climbed up beside me. I was very relieved to see him and his barmy-earthling red anorak.

He was right about the landscape. The strangeness of the Old Testament belonged in this setting: wild, dangerous, with only a thin line keeping pagan demons away from you in solitude. This was where people imagined a god of thunderbolts, fire and vengeance. A landscape too big for human beings to feel safe in.

It wasn't just my overblown imagination that found Petra scary. Rathwan was annoyed by the hustling locals and the strenuous climbing, but its unearthly atmosphere was one of the main reasons why he disliked Petra.

"To be honest the place brings me down. I would hate to be here alone after dark. How people can sleep here . . . Ugh."

I knew what he meant, but Gertrude would have scoffed at us both, I'm sure. She gleefully camped the night among the tombs, and described the brooding edifice of Al-Deir as 'extremely

223

Rococo'. Perhaps Petra had a more jolly, court-of-Louis-Quinze feel in her day.

It's said, among the many things said, that there is ancient treasure hidden somewhere in Petra. Stephen Spielberg knew immediately that Petra was a likely location for Indiana Jones to find the holy grail. Rococo, scary or sacred, Petra is somewhere that people all over the world have in their hearts as a place they yearn to see once in their lives. I hate to pull rank on people all over the world, but I visited Petra five times; I saw it parched dry in summer, carpeted with flowers in spring (wild tulips everywhere before the goats got at them) and snow-coated in winter.

Seeing it with Rathwan was always best, getting drawn inside the local life, sitting around the edge of caves sharing tea and food with Marlboro Boys. We'd watch tourists go by, discuss them, tease some boy who'd taken a shine to a passing foreign girl and egg him on to talk to her. Inevitably, the girl would spurn his advances and the boy would retreat to us, smiling with bravado even though we'd witnessed the rebuff.

The Marlboro Boys were harmlessly, innocently cheeky. The cheekiest spoke English to me with a Yorkshire accent – he'd learnt it from his wife. When he pointed her out, she seemed very happy: she was working as a guide, blonde hair uncovered, riding her camel ahead of her tourists with a glamorous competence; occasionally she'd shout greetings to a local in Arabic that definitely had a tang of Yorkshire. Needless to say, she set me thinking. If Rathwan arranged camel lessons for me . . .

Much as he complained about the place, Rathwan had plenty

of friends in Petra, including the local police, who would entertain us with some of the stranger problems they had with tourists at Petra. Like the time the police went hunting down Dutch visitors because they'd had a tip-off that a group of Dutch people belonging to a bizarre religious sect had chosen Petra as a suitably holy place in which to commit mass suicide. All the Dutch groups had been tracked every inch of their way by the police but there'd been no sign of suicidal behaviour. Rathwan offered to watch out for Dutch people buying Bedouin daggers at souvenir stalls. A keen young policeman, not realising Rathwan was joking, chipped in that his plan was to watch out for Dutch tourists approaching the edge of cliffs – he'd distract them by pretending he'd hurt his leg and needed their help. I pointed out that the police had a fundamental problem: what were they going to do if these people were determined, refused to stop and resisted arrest – shoot them? A net, the young policeman suggested excitedly, we could catch them in a net. An older colleague looked at him wearily: "Suliman," he said, "you are very new."

On our last visit to Petra the worst had happened. The Marlboro Boys had been done away with, only permitted to make pathetic novelty trips of a few hundred yards along a track outside the city. Strange little carts which looked like hospital equipment plied the elderly and infirm through the Siq. The galloping days were over.

Rathwan had to take a group of tourists down to Aqaba, and I was pleased to leave Petra and tag along. But Rathwan felt bad that I'd have to wander around on my own for a couple of days while he was busy with his tourists.

"I will pay for you to stay in a beautiful hotel overlooking the sea. And I've taken the rest of the week off to be with you."

"It's not really fair," I said. "You take all this time off and spend all your money just so I can have a nice holiday. When do you get to go on holiday?"

"When you come here, I feel as though I've been to a completely different place. Everything is so different when you're here, it is my holiday."

It was the sort of thing he said that took the ground from under me and all the future away from me – except the possible future of being in Jordan forever.

The blue seas, palm trees and soft warm sand of Aqaba were a temptation too. I found it easier going than Amman, smaller and more manageable. I could live here, I could be the mad English writer in her house overlooking the bay . . . Except that Aqaba was way off Rathwan's patch; the tribes were very different to his own, the settled people more different still and basically the whole point of revelling beside the seaside escaped him.

He was contented enough as we explored the fort, which had been prettily planted with a central flower garden and didn't look at all as I'd last seen it, being stormed in *Lawrence of Arabia*. And he was only vaguely disconcerted when we went out in a glass-bottomed boat to look at coral reefs and tropical fish:

"They're pretty things, but this man charges too much for his boat. And does he know what he's doing? I'm sure we almost hit that rock."

But on the beach Rathwan was completely miserable. He sat in the shade while I swam and sunbathed, but he'd had enough.

"I have told the waiter in this bar to look after you. If you don't mind I will go back to the hotel to sleep for a couple of hours. Really, I am exhausted."

He may well have been – but he was also desperately uncomfortable. Aqaba beach was full of foreigners and Arab rich kids. Sports cars roared along the corniche, designer sunglasses and beachwear were ubiquitous, and it was the only place in Jordan where I heard Western pop music played on every corner at the same volume as the call of the muezzin. A blonde head was a sight barely worth a second glance in Aqaba, and I could have my arms and legs showing without expecting trouble. So I was generally more at ease, although there were bars and restaurants I felt far too poor and scruffy to set foot in. In one pavement cafe I thought a group of Arab girls might offer me alms once they'd finished showing each other their purchases of Chanel, Gucci, Versace and Everybody-expensive summer wear. Instead, they had a discussion in American-accented English about whether it was 'in' or 'out' to wear gold jewellery with a swimsuit. "Just a touch, you know," one of them said. "Less is like kinda more these days."

Windsurfers scudded around private yachts, there was water-skiing and an open-air disco; it was almost a classy Mediterranean resort. Except that the pot-bellied, bare-chested men sporting Armani sunglasses and bright Bermuda shorts often trailed fully veiled wives. For every slim Arab girl in a bikini by a pool, there was another covered from head to toe under a beach umbrella; for every rich boy playing hip-hop on a ghetto blaster, there was a middle-aged man in traditional Arab dress bowing to Mecca on a prayer mat in the shade.

One evening Rathwan showed me the old part of Aqaba. Right alongside the glitzy hotels and palm-fringed bars, it was like a shanty town, lit by Calor Gas instead of neon and fairy lights. Tourists rarely strayed along its dirt tracks. There were men fixing broken-down cars outside tumble-down little houses, Arab music was playing, and work went on late into the night: gutting fish, baking bread, washing clothes, chopping up goats, strangling chickens . . . servicing the consumers in the other town. People looked at me twice here. Disapprovingly. But Rathwan relaxed, got into conversations with car-fixers and chicken-stranglers. He was in charge again, as we bought kebabs from a busy stall; at home, as he joked with some children who were trying to sell us dirty postcards – 'dirty' in the sense that they looked like they'd been buried for a couple of years.

There was the key to our problem then: I felt like a poor relation but definitely at ease in the Mediterranean atmosphere of Aqaba; Rathwan, on the other hand, remained twitchy until we were back in Downtown Amman.

The night before I was to return to London we sat up late in the Hotel Wadi lounge, having a laughing conversation about the British royal family, among many other topics. Rathwan thought it ludicrous that there were so many British royals with wealth so unimaginably far above that of even their better-off subjects. There were plenty of people in Jordan who were richer than King

Hussein. He looked richer than he was because of all the stuff he needed to be king – palaces, a plane, helicopters, staff, guards . . . But Hussein's personal wealth was very small potatoes. And he earned his keep, by ruling. Rathwan didn't understand why we tolerated our ridiculously wealthy queen when she wasn't even doing anything useful like running the country. I astounded him further by recounting the antics of Charles, Di, Fergie and the rest. Why didn't we run them into the sea? What were we scared of? They were as corrupt and dissolute as the Al-Sabahs, but unlike their Kuwaiti counterparts our royals had no flogging and execution rights over their rebellious subjects. Why put up with them then? What was wrong with the British?

Amjad brought us tea around midnight. Rathwan told him I was leaving in the morning, and Amjad's smile dropped away in confusion.

"*Laysh*?" he asked me. Why?

"It's my work," I told him in Arabic, and he returned to his kitchen, not looking entirely satisfied with my explanation.

"So your Arabic is getting better," Rathwan commented.

"No thanks to you, Mr Impatient." He was a dreadful teacher, baffled that I took so long to grasp things, nit-pickingly insistent on correct pronunciation.

"I prefer it when you speak English. The way you speak is like magic. I can see why you are a writer. I understand why people like how you use words."

"I wish more people thought that – I'd be rich."

"Perhaps you will be. In some ways, I wish you didn't have this writing. It's what takes you away."

"If I didn't have it I wouldn't be me."

"No. Of course not," he sighed. "You know, you have destroyed me for anyone else. Whatever happens I couldn't love anyone else like this."

An extraordinary diversion stopped me bursting into tears in front of the Iraqis who'd just arrived in the lounge and were squabbling ferociously over which television channel to watch. Amjad came running down the back stairs dragging an enormous black garbage sack behind him – which burst, scattering its contents. Women's clothes, including a particularly splendid pair of gold stiletto shoes. I had wondered if Amjad had a private life, but . . . He grabbed up his belongings, flustered.

The explanation wasn't that exciting: "Amjad is to be married in Egypt next month. These are gifts for his wife."

Mahmoud sprang from his office, chivvied Amjad to hurry himself out of the way, switched off the television and confiscated the remote control.

"I am doing accounts, Han. They must be quiet. No quiet, no switcher." He slammed back into his office leaving us all staring at the blank screen.

One of the older Iraqis, who obviously thought it was a little beneath his dignity to be punished like a schoolboy by a young pup like Mahmoud, got up and hammered on the office door, bellowing as only an Iraqi can.

Mahmoud grumped out again and, after more bellowing, entrusted the older man with responsibility for the remote control. Suddenly, Mahmoud swung round to look at me crossly. What had I done?

"Han. Tomorrow you go?" Mahmoud asked, as if he was sure I had all the family silver and switchers packed in my case.

"Yes, tomorrow."

"It no good, Han. Go come go. You must have stay. Stay. One two three every day. Finish!"

CHAPTER 8

Very Modern Art, Very Old Culture

Rathwan frowned. "What's it supposed to be?"

A bit like Henry Moore, I thought.

It's difficult enough to get someone enthused about modern art when they know nothing at all about it, but when the works you're making them look at are lifeless and derivative, it's very hard to defend your own fanaticism. Nevertheless I tried, raving on at Rathwan about colour and form, about how you were just supposed to like what you saw, like the feeling you get from looking at a beautiful view . . . He was now standing in front of a pretentious imitation of a European style, a mash of expression in purple. He stared harder at it.

"But it's ugly," he said.

I was so disappointed. I had thought the longstanding tradition of non-representation in Islamic art would mean I'd see something wonderful, of itself. Instead I saw artists who'd studied abroad and lost their direction. Rathwan had thought he'd discover why I was always hankering to visit an art gallery; all he discovered was snippy gallery attendants looking at him the way the worst of city people could peer down their noses at Bedouin. And then there were the ghastly objects I was asking him to appreciate . . .

On the way out, we passed a cube of concrete with a hole in it. Rathwan circled it disdainfully.

"I think you made a mistake. This is not in the exhibition, it is something to sit on."

I showed him the tag on the wall. The sculpture was called *Untitled*, which involved a lengthy explanation in itself, and was by a young Saudi. Rathwan squinted at it.

"He didn't feel shy when he made this?"

"Oh no! What a terrible thing to happen!" Rathwan exclaimed as he read his newspaper over breakfast. "There is an art exhibition today at the Goethe Institut." A few years had passed since his unsuccessful encounter with modern art, but he hadn't forgotten the experience.

"Aha!" I grabbed at the paper to check the details.

He sighed. "I will be made to go, I expect."

And I expected he would go just about anywhere that he thought would humour me. Seeing as he'd just got married, to someone else.

For months there'd been something funny in his voice on the phone. A hesitation. Even when we were confirming my flight details, I'd thought there was a top note missing from his excitement.

When I arrived, I could tell he was pleased to see me; I could also tell there was something wrong. As soon as our taxi left the airport rank, he tore the words out of himself:

"Annie, something has happened."

There was no other thought that came to me.

"You got married."

"How did you know?"

"I just knew."

"I didn't tell you. I wanted you to see my eyes when I told you. On the telephone . . . If I told you on the telephone perhaps you'd never come back."

He pleaded with me to believe that the marriage had been forced on him. Otherwise he'd have been publicly denounced by his father and his uncles, his precarious tie to his family and culture severed. There'd even been threats from an uncle who knew the Minister of Tourism to get his guide permit revoked. He'd been forced. I had to understand that, forced.

She was twenty-seven, the daughter of a friend of his father's, a Bedouin girl. I wondered, fleetingly, how much she'd been forced too. But she'd got herself a kind, good-looking catch. Never mind her.

"Believe me, Annie, I don't like this girl. I certainly don't love her. I don't even like her."

"What's wrong with her?"

Please let her be hideous, mad . . .

"There's nothing wrong with her, but she isn't you. There is no feeling there. It's just something that happened. She means nothing."

I had a pang of guilt. Some poor girl thinking she had a marriage and her husband was saying this to someone else.

"There is no feeling there, Annie. This is what I want you to know. It is you in my heart and if I lose you . . ."

"I expected it."

Of course I had. It was foreshadowed in everything I'd ever read or heard about relationships like ours; it was part of everything that had held me back from marrying him myself. At the same time, I knew he was telling me the truth. "As long as we're still the same, your marriage doesn't matter to me."

His taut pain vanished and his whole being seemed to smile.

"I loved you before, but now, when you say this, I love you even more. I was afraid you would hate me, and you would be right to. But now I know we'll always survive."

I really didn't feel a thing. I was so certain this marriage of his was a minor irritation, an irrelevance. But the significance and power of this irrelevance gradually began to make itself felt. By the end of the first week, as he left the Hotel Wadi early, yet again, to go home to his wife, I started to kick round my room, spitting feathers and wishing seven kinds of hell on her.

Rathwan's answer was to offer me the post of second wife. Even for that, we needed to wait until a decent interval had passed. This marriage of his was starting to have all the irrelevance to my life of the ground opening up under my feet. All of a sudden Rathwan was serious about his religion; the notion of adultery terrified him. From being understanding and gracious, I snapped into a recurring scream at him, shrieking accusations without sense or dignity. So, suddenly his soul mattered to him now he was getting it at home? Why didn't he tell her about me? How come her feelings had to be protected because she was a stupid ignorant lump while I had to cope with all the pain? How come she got everything for nothing, but I'd spent years crossing the world to see him and ended up losing him?

He begged, cried and kept telling me how much more important I was. How he hadn't even known he mattered that much to me. How could he have, when I'd been evasive and uncertain, rejecting even, for years?

"You know I wanted it to be you that was my wife before God and before all the people. But I knew you would never marry me."

"You didn't know. I needed more time."

"There wasn't any time. I'd already kept them waiting too long. I could have lost all my family and my place here. I had to decide. I decided not to wait because you never said anything to make me wait."

"So that's it? I had my chance and I've missed it?"

"I'm not saying that. Don't ever think that. I still need you."

"So you get everything that suits you? Your Bedouin respectability as well as me. A second wife."

"It can be like before. You come and go but you are equal to her. You're more than equal."

Except that he wouldn't be able to tell anyone I was his wife. It was a very small country, especially his strand of it. Eventually word would get back to the desert.

"Don't worry," he said, trying to end one of many arguments.

"We won't be separated. You are in my heart. God will give us the solution."

In my view, God was responsible for a good deal of the problem and certainly wouldn't be handing out solutions to unbelievers like me. Rathwan, however, had taken up praying. He said it kept him sane. Something in the way Muslims prayed, the regular meditative break spaced throughout the day, the repetition of set phrases, the whole body involved in the simple physical rituals – the process itself could focus and balance you when you felt your life was a screaming unravelment all around you. Like stopping to take long, deep breaths.

He had changed – as if half the guts had been kicked out of him. He had always been so confident that he could live on his wits and not bother to fret where the next dinar might be coming from. Now he worried about money all the time. He was compelled to work as much as he could, hustling to get taken on by one of the new firms specialising in trips for the Israeli tourists who'd come pouring in since King Hussein signed a peace treaty with that country.

I reminded Rathwan of what he'd once said about Israel not existing. "There's peace now," he growled at me. "Anyway, business is business."

So never mind that he talked with Ismat and other Palestinians about how this peace felt like the Palestinians were being sold down the river to make it happen. Not that there was much time for hanging around Ismat's house setting the world to rights or clowning around with the boys till all hours. He had to hurry home, catching a bus every evening to his village and his wife, queuing up with the other tired, shuffling workers. Rathwan, who'd always hated buses.

Sadness for Rathwan held back my anger after a while of watching his new life. And he was so good to me in those weeks after his confession. Any spare time he had was given over to me, anything I wanted to do he tried to arrange for me.

He took me to the exhibition at the Goethe Institut, for instance. I was interested in it because the artist was a Palestinian woman. Rathwan was interested because as soon as we went into the building, he saw shapes on canvas he recognised. There were pictures of old men mending shoes on Jerusalem side-streets that I liked, but I had to conclude that the old men must be early work and she'd since had a talent extraction in some hospital mix-up. Her other paintings were hideous: horses, flowers, kittens . . . Garish, chocolate-boxy things that would put you off chocolates for life if you found them on your box.

Rathwan was immensely taken with them all. Heartened by the experience, he decided to accompany me to the national gallery of fine arts.

"The things you showed me before were terrible, Annie. But now I've seen this woman's paintings I think I can share this interest with you."

The gallery was in an old part of Amman where there were yellow, sandstone houses with carved balconies surrounded by trees. A nice quiet part of town to live in . . . Rathwan noticed me admiring the houses but said nothing.

En route, we met up with Bashir, who was off duty for the

afternoon. The idea of making a special trip to see paintings was strange and amusing to him.

"Open your mind, Bashir!" Rathwan said.

"I'm here, aren't I? My mind is closed but I am looking from my window."

The gallery was somewhat run-down, but it was a pleasant enough place, brightly lit, with white stone walls and wooden floors. Wooden benches were dotted around, and Bashir and Rathwan made full use of them after a lot of exaggerated checking that they weren't going to sit on art. Most of the work on display was abstract; most of it, at first glance, was disappointing. Rathwan and Bashir behaved like naughty schoolboys, whispering and giggling when my back was turned, then staring with mock intensity at paintings when 'Miss' swung around. I hadn't realised that I was peering and aha-ing pretentiously, like a character in a Woody Allen film, until I caught them mimicking me.

Standing in front of a huge, would-be-cubist pink business, Rathwan asked despairingly, "But Annie, what is good about this?"

There was a moment of excited hope when they found two charcoal drawings of camels, from Mongolia. Bashir pointed to it, beaming: "Aha!"

"Aha! Now this . . ." Rathwan sighed appreciatively. "Camels, look. Heads, legs, feet . . ."

Consternation followed swiftly when Bashir pointed out that the camels had two humps each. Despair. Not even a decent straightforward drawing of a camel. I explained that Mongolian camels have two humps. They didn't believe me.

"Have you been to Mongolia?" Rathwan asked scathingly.

"No, but I've seen them in a zoo."

He didn't look convinced.

"Honestly. They're called Bactrian camels."

"Hmm. I think they're called modern art camels."

And they sat out the rest of the exhibition, remaining unimpressed even when I spotted some powerful work from Iraq and the Sudan – proof that everything I'd imagined about the Arab world being the true home of abstract art hadn't been merely the ravings of a madwoman who didn't know a two-humped camel from her elbow.

The art obsession wasn't something I'd thought up purely as a torment for Rathwan and his friends. In the middle of all our emotional disaster, I was trying to make a radio programme about Jordanian culture. This work was much more than just a job now, it was a vital distraction I needed to fill in the hours when Rathwan couldn't be with me. I'd arrange an interview and he'd send me off with notes in Arabic to show cab drivers in case I forgot the address or my bad pronunciation stumped them; he'd also check that I was carrying the Hotel Wadi's flashy gold card at all times. I felt like an evacuee child or Paddington Bear – 'If lost, please return this blonde to . . .'

The funny thing was, I began to meet people who could have opened up a whole new world for me; I began to see how I could live an independent life in Jordan that wouldn't be too different from the one I led at home. Rathwan had always told me this – that there were people 'of my kind' I could meet in Jordan:

writers, actors, painters, theatre directors, people from the fledgling film industry. Belatedly, I realised I didn't always have to leave a part of myself behind in London.

Worse still, I'd meet up with Rathwan in the evening and he'd be full of delighted interest in my interviewing adventures; then he'd tell me if he'd seen anyone we knew or if funny things had happened with his tourists that day. This was how our marriage might have been if I'd been a little braver. No. If I'd had time to find out what I was discovering when it was too late.

Just when I'd lost him, I was seeing so much about his country. *Because* I'd lost him and could step out of his view of the landscape.

"These tribal people will be the last to change," a big, confident woman with her own design business told me. "Women's lives change from the top down. But there *is* change – especially in the middle classes." She sighed: "Freedom is a matter of economics. Isn't it always so, my dear?"

Of course. If I hadn't had the education that enabled me to earn my own living . . . And Gertrude would never have had her exceptional adventures if she hadn't been from a rich and influential family. Maybe Rathwan's wife had notions of places she'd like to go, things she dreamt of doing . . . Never mind her.

"I try to help women's lives, even in a trivial thing like fashion I think there are ways to combine modesty with chic. But the women who can't afford my clothes are stuck wearing those bundles of cloth. But isn't it the same in your country? The lower classes seem more conservative because they have less opportunity for choice."

'The lower classes . . .' 'These tribal people . . .' Although I was enjoying being introduced into rarefied circles as the girl from the BBC, circles Rathwan couldn't have introduced me to, I knew he'd shown me a Jordan I would only have seen from a distance if I'd gone in armed with just my BBC credentials.

I interviewed a novelist in the coffee shop of the Amman Intercontinental hotel, which was something of a hangout for both the intelligentsia and the smart set; we drank cappuccino and talked about the changing form of the Arab novel. In the foyer was a *tableau vivant* of Bedouin life: a man wearing full Bedouin dress was standing by a fake fire surrounded by stuffed goats; using traditional coffee-making equipment, he was making cups of coffee to welcome hotel guests.

"I hope he's an actor," I said when I told Rathwan about it.

"Of course he's an actor," came the reply. "A real Bedouin would feel sick to do this."

Rathwan's life was real, current and it was also folklore.

We had giggled over a ridiculous and extremely expensive trip visitors could take along the Hejaz railway – the one Lawrence and his Bedouin band blew up. These days the line was used largely for freight, but there were special excursions for those with the price of a ticket. These privileged passengers travelled on the railway through the Wadi Rum desert; a man in a white tuxedo played a grand piano while guests drank champagne and nibbled on canapés. Then a group of armed, mounted Bedouin staged a mock raid on the train. Afterwards, coffee was served with liqueurs as the Bedouin galloped away into the sunset.

"I expect they get good pay for this raid. But I don't know if it's really funny or not," Rathwan had said. Guiding tourists was one thing; making a circus out of an ongoing way of life and a proudly remembered historical event might be quite another. Rathwan's people trod a lot of fine lines.

Rather embarrassingly for my own fine lines, I discovered that so many local artists had gone to live among the Bedouin, looking for inspiration, that the idea was considered a dreadful cliché.

"I think it's like in Australia," a writer said to me. "They've killed most of the Aborigines but now discovered they're these great artists and mystically spiritual people. I don't know about the Bedouin being great artists, and we didn't kill them of course, but Arabs who've lived all their lives in the city romanticise about the strength of Bedouin tradition, their freedom of spirit, the glories of life out in the desert. They go and hang around the Bedouin, painting them and writing about them. Not that any of them would really want to live like a Bedouin forever."

I nodded. Said nothing.

The dichotomy between old and new dominated the work of writers in Jordan. One playwright told me of a piece she'd written about the heartbreaking way a woman's spirit had been crushed through an arranged marriage; she then went on to talk about the project she was working on, a comic satire on the way Jordanians were turning themselves inside out in their effort to be Western. I made her laugh, describing the American accents and Monte Carlo behaviour I'd seen in Aqaba.

"Exactly," she said. "And what these people don't know is

how silly they look to you. We must celebrate our own culture."

Tricky, she agreed, to determine how much that culture depended on women remaining the same put upon, hidden creatures.

"This society," she concluded, "wants to move on but doesn't want to let go of the past in case it becomes . . . just floating, like a soap bubble with its entire shape created by the air currents around it. Do you see what I mean?"

I was beginning to.

"You must understand the insecurity here," another writer told me. "In the Middle East even your nationality isn't a certainty. You can be a Palestinian one day and in Israel the next. You can go to bed in Kuwait and wake up in part of Iraq. You can be an Iraqi all your life and then have to find somewhere else to live for the rest of your days. And here, in Jordan, who knows if we'll be a country tomorrow? It's harder for us to play with our heritage because we also need to cling to it, to whatever pieces we have."

When some of my new journalist friends dropped me off at the Hotel Wadi one evening, they were fairly surprised by my choice of accommodation.

"How else would I get to see the authentic life of Jordan?" seemed the easiest explanation.

"Oh, this place is authentic all right," one of them laughed.

The extremely authentic Mahmoud was watching 'Sesame Street' with great relish the next morning.

"Han! You have these things in England?"

We did. Although the forcefulness of Arabic seemed particularly suited to these fractious puppets.

A very hairy, indeed muppet-like old Iraqi in a corner of the lounge growled out from behind his newspaper: "Sesame Street! What happened to Shakespeare? Is he out now?"

The relative merits of muppets and Shakespeare was not a pressing concern for an Iraqi artist I was introduced to later that day. A journalist friend had tracked the artist down for me after I'd admired his work in Amman's new arts centre, Darat Al-Funun.

Darat Al-Funun was the name given to the centre by King Hussein and meant 'little house of art'. It was a particularly attractive house; originally the home of a leading Jordanian family in the 1920s, it was also where T.E. Lawrence wrote a great deal of *Seven Pillars of Wisdom*. Carefully preserving the elegant style of the original architecture, Darat Al-Funun provided gallery space, studios and promotional assistance for the best of the Arab world's established painters along with the talented up-and-comers. The work being carried out and exhibited here was richly varied and exciting. Iraqis dominated the exhibitions as so many of them had fled to Jordan to work in peace and safety. But they weren't taken on by the centre as charity cases – thousands of years of artistic tradition punched through their complex paintings.

"I come from a very old school," the artist I admired reminded me. "Mesopotamia, this is how far back we're talking."

But in his recent past his creativity had all but suffocated in Iraq; there was no hope for those who wouldn't take on work for the glorification of Saddam's regime. Direct dissidence was suicidal. Even Jordan wasn't really far enough away for those who were actively critical of Saddam Hussein; the dictator had umpteen kinds of secret police, so it was reasonable to assume some of them must be sneaking about among the Iraqis in Jordan. I wondered who in the Hotel Wadi lounge . . . ?

With the help of free exhibition space at Darat Al-Funun, my artist friend was hoping to finance a move to Paris. "It will be good to work in a city that isn't ugly. Baghdad has been made very ugly. People are starving, there was the bombing damage in the Gulf War. Also Saddam is obsessed with building enormous monuments to himself. Nothing is constructed that doesn't have his face or his initials somewhere. I find it astonishing, don't you? That one man's ego can ruin the lives of so many people."

"So what do the Iraqis do?" I asked him. "Wait for Saddam to die or be assassinated?"

He shrugged, waning from anger to depression. "Did you ever read that book about the Roman emperors, *I, Claudius*? Believe me, that's how it is. What's coming after Saddam will only be worse. Sadism and madness like nothing we've seen yet."

I bought cigarettes and toys from every Iraqi woman I passed on the pavement on my way to meet Rathwan at the Roman theatre. Predictably, my head was running with those lines from *Casablanca* about the problems of two little people not amounting to a hill of beans . . .

I was early so I wandered into the folklore museum housed in a wing of the theatre. I'd been there before but never noticed the particular exhibit I found myself staring at that afternoon. It was as if some friend of Rathwan's wife had snuck in and put it there to spite me. The taunting display was of elaborate paper puppets on sticks; they were used in satirical and often vulgar shows that originated in the tenth-century Fatimid era and remained popular until quite recently. The exhibition samples were from the nineteenth century, when a favourite butt of the puppeteers' humour was the growing number of Western Orientalists pestering the Middle East. Notorious pests were English women, who made up the majority of the *ferrengi* (foreign women) cavorting obsessively around the region. Women like Hester Stanhope, or the one represented in the theatre museum as a daft-looking creature wearing a daft hat, Isobel Burton.

So there was another cliché I'd become: mad *ferrengi* thinks she's got inside Middle Eastern life and doesn't realise how much she's sniggered at behind her back. Fool.

Thank God I didn't wear a hat.

Rathwan stood at the airport barrier as always, watching for every last chance to wave goodbye to me. Well, I hoped she was happy, that Bedouin girl, she had a great husband. I had a ticket home and a small, intricate Hebron glass vase I'd bought as a souvenir because I'd decided I was never going back.

I didn't tell Rathwan. He'd been so desperate, had promised that I'd still be his wife, that I was the one who really mattered. But the religion he invoked, now that he had an alternative to adultery, had done it for me. And there was something pathetic about his fear of being cut off from his family, when most of

247

them, including his father, had never shown him even basic kindness.

There were probably reasons and explanations to find in his miserable childhood and Artful Dodger adolescence, some long-felt desperation to belong. To rebel, cut loose and go solo was so normal in my world, but it was a frighteningly lonely path to carve out in his gregarious, family-centred environment. So, on the one hand, I did understand. On the other, there were the long evenings I had to spend alone at the Hotel Wadi because he had to get home early enough to make it look like he'd been at work. And the lonely days when he was working, earning money for his wife and her household, while I'd spent money I'd earned myself to be with him. Finally there was the image of a girl seven years my junior wearing gold he'd given her, gloating around the tents with him in tow when she went out visiting. I didn't know if she had the kind of life where she got to do a lot of visiting and gloating, but I was sure that if the chance came along she'd being doing just that. I knew Rathwan, I knew that no matter what he really felt – or rather because of his real feelings – his kindness and decency would ensure he was very, very nice to her.

With a mawkish irony that would have set a cinema audience groaning, my departure scene was accompanied by the airport muzak suddenly switching to a medley of Western tunes: 'La Vie en Rose', followed by – I promise you –'Auld Lang Syne'; my flight was called just as Harry Nilsson's 'Without You' was taking me from the verge of tears to an abject sobbing that I couldn't have seen an end to, had I let it start.

Seven hours later, I settled down to a quiet stream of tears in my empty little flat and began to unpack the pieces of Hebron vase my dirty clothes hadn't adequately protected. Just as worldly cynicism and common sense hadn't protected my heart from smashing up. I flung myself down on my bed and howled, like a Bedouin girl in a soap opera. Except that this was real and it really hurt.

CHAPTER 9

Final Cut

But . . . As Gertrude said, 'It was one of those long stories that you hear in the East, without beginning, without end, and without any indication as to which of the protagonists is in the right, but an inherent probability that all are in the wrong.'

In the weeks that followed, my mind didn't just change forty times a minute about Rathwan's marriage – it flew across my skull and then bounced off in the opposite direction, the way a cartoon animal bounces off the walls, floor and ceiling of a room after it's been flung with huge force by some enemy: *kerrang! kerrang! kerrang!* Eventually exhausted, the animal would slide down the wall and give up the fight. I longed to reach that stage. To just forget the whole business. Then – *kerrang!* I'd fly out fighting again.

I wanted something to happen to make Rathwan's wife cry. I wanted to find out where she lived, go and tell her everything, and maybe poke her eyes out with the stick end of a *ferrengi* puppet.

Then I'd remember the pang I'd felt in my heart when I heard Alia had been married off to a man she didn't know. And not to whoever she'd been whispering and giggling over the night we had our fortunes told. Did Rathwan's wife have someone else she'd hoped for as a husband? Someone who loved her more than Rathwan ever could?

I'd repeatedly mentioned to Rathwan the tale of a nineteenth-century *ferrengi* that I'd read with great interest. Jane Digby fell in love with a sheikh; he divorced his Arab wife for her and they lived happily ever after. But Rathwan wouldn't divorce his wife – it would be too cruel, he told me, what had she done to deserve it? Well, tough.

The dreams of the havoc and destruction I'd wreak on his wife's world began to perturb me – how much of the urge was simply to do with my being a walking definition of vanity? I was imagining all kinds of dreadful tricks I might play to ensure I was the 'winner' over some poor girl who didn't even know there was a contest. Really, the sort of bad ego problems that make charmers like Saddam Hussein.

Rathwan didn't rush in heroically with a decisive plan of action. He was caught, like so many of the protagonists in Arab fiction, between all the strands of belief in his head. The Bedouin traditions he was so proud of had made him abandon his personal pride and desires in order to meet their demands. The religion that tormented his conscience when he was with me also gave him the option of polygamy so that we could be together – an option he was prepared to take up for my sake. Yet I knew from conversations we'd had over the years that he didn't believe in taking more than one wife, always citing the hurt and neglect in his father's polygamous household as the reason. If he married me he'd be starting to turn into his father.

I thought about how Gertrude's love story had ended. The man she was in love with was quite fond of her, until she cracked one day and begged him to leave his wife. Taken by surprise, he politely declined and suggested they'd best not meet again. A few weeks later, he was killed at Gallipoli; an affair that could have died so romantically in her imagination had already been buried under a weight of humiliation.

This time I didn't want to be anything like poor Gertrude. Such a good girl, so patient and so discreet – until the impetuous moment when she spoke up for herself, she was everything a mistress should be. Mistress was the word for a second wife in my culture and meek discretion really wasn't the life for a truculent creature like me.

To avoid tragedy or the whole thing being just a loss of our time, we became friends.

'If I thought I'd never see you again it would destroy me', Rathwan had written at the end of an unusually long letter.

The thought of never meeting and giggling together again was something I couldn't stand either. I forgot that I was never going back and did go back. Just to talk to Rathwan – that's what we always did so well.

Eventually we become like two Arab boys whose friendship was full of ambiguous physical affection, only a heartbeat away from the sexual. It wasn't easy. I felt like he'd stabbed a sharp

Bedouin dagger in my back when he told me his wife had had a baby. I was sure he'd punch a breeze block out of his house if I ever got married or even fell in love with someone else. But it was still better to leave it like this than have one of us ending up all pulled out of shape and turning sour with trying to leave our culture behind to please the other.

Though we'd probably not make the expedition we'd planned tracing Gertrude's route or go to Baghdad together or even find out about our lunatic who walked Amman in his cardboard crown, we already had plenty of reasons to ask each other, "Do you remember . . . ?" And be off into some old private joke.

When I nervously showed him a draft manuscript of this book, he said, "It's OK. Now I know what you were thinking all the time." Then he smiled. "But I see you didn't know what I was thinking."

Was there anything in it he didn't like?

"I'm not sure about this part where you go on about Bashir and Salah looking like film stars in leather boots."

"I say you have eyes like Omar Sharif."

"But he is an old man. And I see you return again to the matter of you being shot at. This is so like you. Whenever I argue with you, you bring up all the old injuries. We could argue now about this book and you'll be throwing things into the argument that I did wrong four years ago."

"I don't do that."

"I can give you instances stretching back four years. Anyway writing books is not my business, it's not for me to comment."

"But if there's something you really don't like in the book . . ."

"There's lots of things. But I expect you know best, you with your hair like a sheep."

Whether or not I knew best became uncertain as a multitude of details I'd left out of our story occurred to me. Like the time Abu Hamdi boasted he had a tape of 'English music' and played a cassette that could only be described as the soundtrack from a wildlife programme. Or the day we'd travelled up to Umm Qais and looked out over the Sea of Galilee and the Golan Heights. When I told Rathwan that Christians believed Jesus had walked on the sea through a storm, he thought it was the funniest thing he'd ever heard.

"Christians believe this story?"

"Religious people do."

Coming from a man who always instinctively turned shoes the right way up so that their soles weren't facing heaven and insulting God, someone who picked pieces of bread off the ground in case they were trodden on in an insult to God's providence, Rathwan's scepticism seemed to me very much a case of the salt-thrower calling the wood-toucher superstitious.

There was the time I'd insisted that I'd nearly drowned in the Dead Sea. I'd been floating and kicking around in the water for a couple of hours and gone out quite far, when Rathwan called out that it was time for lunch. I swam and swam through the salt porridge, and started to have a genuine panic attack that I'd never get out. As I'd panted and blubbered up to him, Rathwan had just laughed.

"But Annie no one can drown in the Dead Sea – that's the point."

"I nearly bloody did! So shut up!"

Later that day we'd visited an old Bedouin aunt of his – so many tribal tattoos she'd a face like a biker's arm. She told Rathwan I was much nicer than the other foreign girls she'd seen: I dressed modestly and wasn't always shouting – the foreign girl who'd married into her village was forever losing her temper and shouting.

"Oh no, Annie never shouts," Rathwan had said, smirking at me.

There was Umm al-Jimal, where we'd seen two male camels have a ferocious biting, kicking fight over an insouciant female. Tafila, in the Southern Desert, where the people were all said to be mad from inbreeding; Rathwan would always threaten to leave me there in the middle of the night when I gave him a hard time. Mount Nebo, where Moses had been shown the promised land and I'd got a spontaneous nosebleed for the first time in my life – hopefully, an event of no theological significance.

"Mukawir. You forgot Mukawir."

Yes, there was Mukawir or Machaerus, Herod's palace over-looking the Dead Sea, where Salome had danced for the head of John the Baptist. And Madaba, Pella, Salt . . . All the places we'd seen together, the length and breadth of the country.

Rathwan said that images of us flashed through his mind all the time. I wondered how many of them were the same as mine, if we were ever re-running the same favourite scene at the same time.

But I had some secret scenes, my director's cut of things I remembered as being typical of him.

Like his reaction when we'd looked at a red Corvette convertible in Aqaba.

"Nice, isn't it?" I'd pined.

"No. If it turns over, your brain is straight onto the road. No, I don't like those things, I've never liked them."

The mysterious way his clothes always looked meticulously clean and uncrumpled, even after days in the desert; how he'd fold back his shirt sleeves when eating, fold them very precisely not just roll them, and then carefully readjust them when he'd finished, checking minutely to make sure they were straight and unblemished.

His inability to pass a poor child or a beggar without giving them some money with a subtlety that was almost sleight of hand.

There was the time I realised my Arabic had improved far more than he knew. As he watched me walk across an open-air cafe towards him, I heard him mutter under his breath, "God, she's so beautiful."

It had all been worth it, to a walking definition of vanity, to have a memory like that.

LONELY PLANET JOURNEYS

JOURNEYS is a unique collection of travellers' tales – published by the company that understands travel better than anyone else.

It is a series for anyone who has ever experienced – or dreamed of – the magical moment when they encountered a strange culture or saw a place for the first time. They are tales to read while you're planning a trip, while you're on the road or while you're in an armchair, in front of a fire.

Lonely Planet guidebooks have always gone beyond providing simple nuts-and-bolts information, so it is a short step to JOURNEYS, a new series of outstanding titles that will explore our planet through the eyes of a fascinating and diverse group of international travellers.

JOURNEYS books will catch the spirit of a place, illuminate a culture, recount a crazy adventure, or introduce a fascinating way of life. They will always entertain, and always enrich the experience of travel.

FULL CIRCLE

A South American Journey

Luis Sepúlveda (translated by Chris Andrews)

'A journey without a fixed itinerary' in the company of Chilean writer Luis Sepúlveda. Extravagant characters and extraordinary situations are memorably evoked: gauchos organising a tournament of lies, a scheming heiress on the lookout for a husband, a pilot with a corpse on board his plane . . . Part autobiography, part travel memoir, *Full Circle* brings us the distinctive voice of one of South America's most compelling writers.

WINNER 1996 Astrolabe – Etonnants Voyageurs award for the best work of travel literature published in France.

THE GATES OF DAMASCUS
Lieve Joris (translated by Sam Garrett)

This best-selling book is a beautifully drawn portrait of day-to-day life in modern Syria. Through her intimate contact with local people, Lieve Joris draws us into the fascinating world that lies behind the gates of Damascus. Hala's husband is a political prisoner, jailed for his opposition to the Assad regime; through the author's friendship with Hala we see how Syrian politics impacts on the lives of ordinary people.

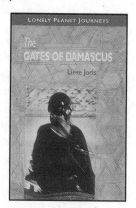

Written after the Gulf War, *The Gates of Damascus* offers a unique insight into the complexities of the Arab world.

IN RAJASTHAN
Royina Grewal

As she writes of her travels through Rajasthan, Indian writer Royina Grewal takes us behind the exotic facade of this fabled destination: here is an insider's perceptive account of India's most colourful state. *In Rajasthan* discusses folk music and architecture, feudal traditions and regional cuisine . . . Most of all, it focuses on people – from maharajas to camel trainers, from politicians to itinerant snake charmers – to convey the excitement and challenges of a region in transition.

ISLANDS IN THE CLOUDS
Travels in the Highlands of New Guinea
Isabella Tree

This is the fascinating account of a journey to the remote and beautiful Highlands of Papua New Guinea and Irian Jaya: one of the most extraordinary and dangerous regions on the planet. The author travels with a PNG Highlander who introduces her to his intriguing and complex world, which is changing rapidly as it collides with twentieth-century technology and the island's developing social and political systems. *Islands in the Clouds* is a thoughtful, moving book, full of insights into a region that is rarely noticed by the rest of the world.

LOST JAPAN
Alex Kerr

Lost Japan draws on the author's personal experiences of Japan over thirty years. Alex Kerr takes his readers on a backstage tour, exploring different facets of his involvement with the country: friendships with Kabuki actors, buying and selling art, studying calligraphy, exploring rarely visited temples and shrines . . .

The Japanese edition of this book was awarded the 1994 Shincho Gakugei Literature Prize for the best work of non-fiction: the first time a foreigner has won this prestigious award.

SEAN & DAVID'S LONG DRIVE

Sean Condon

Sean and David are young townies who have rarely strayed beyond city limits. One day, for no good reason, they set out to discover their homeland, and what follows is a wildly entertaining adventure that covers half of Australia. Highlights include the weekly Hair Wax Report and a Croc-Spotting with Stew adventure.

Sean Condon has written a hilarious, offbeat road book that mixes sharp insights with deadpan humour and outright lies.

SHOPPING FOR BUDDHAS

Jeff Greenwald

'Here in this distant, exotic land, we were compelled to raise the art of shopping to an experience that was, on the one hand, almost Zen – and, on the other hand, tinged with desperation like shopping at Macy's or Bloomingdale's during a one-day-only White Sale.'

Shopping for Buddhas is Jeff Greenwald's story of his obsessive search for the perfect Buddha statue. In the backstreets of Kathmandu, he discovers more than he bargained for . . . and his souvenir-hunting turns into an ironic metaphor for the clash between spiritual riches and material greed. Politics, religion and serious shopping collide in this witty account of an enlightening visit to Nepal.

RELATED TITLES
FROM LONELY PLANET

Jordan & Syria – a travel survival kit

Explore the ruins of rare civilisations, ride a camel across the Wadi Rum desert or snorkel some of the finest coral reefs in the world in the Gulf of Aqaba. This practical guide offers travellers the opportunity to get off the beaten track and experience traditional Arab hospitality.

Middle East on a shoestring

All the travel advice and essential information for travel in Afghanistan, Bahrain, Egypt, Iran, Iraq, Israel, Jordan, Kuwait, Lebanon, Oman, Qatar, Saudi Arabia, Syria, Turkey, United Arab Emirates and Yemen.

Arabic (Egyptian) phrasebook

This phrasebook is full of essential words and phrases that cover almost every situation. The inclusion of Arabic script makes this book useful for travellers visiting other Arabic-speaking countries.

Also available:

Arab Gulf States, Egypt & the Sudan, Iran, Israel, Trekking in Turkey, Turkey, Yemen, Turkish phrasebook & Jordan, Syria & Lebanon travel atlas

PLANET TALK

Lonely Planet's FREE quarterly newsletter

Every issue of PLANET TALK is packed with
up-to-date travel news and advice including:

- a letter from Lonely Planet founders Tony
  and Maureen Wheeler
- travel diary from a Lonely Planet author
  – find out what it's really like out on the road
- feature article on an important and topical
  travel issue
- a selection of recent letters from our readers
- the latest travel news from all over the world
- details on Lonely Planet's new and
  forthcoming releases

To join our mailing list contact any Lonely Planet office.

LONELY PLANET PUBLICATIONS

Australia: PO Box 617, Hawthorn 3122, Victoria
tel: (03) 9819 1877 fax: (03) 9819 6459
e-mail: talk2us@lonelyplanet.com.au

USA: Embarcadero West, 155 Filbert St, Suite 251,
Oakland, CA 94607
tel: (510) 893 8555 TOLL FREE: 800 275-8555
fax: (510) 893 8563 e-mail: info@lonelyplanet.com

UK: 10 Barley Mow Passage, Chiswick, London W4 4PH
tel: (0181) 742 3161 fax: (0181) 742 2772
e-mail: 100413.3551@compuserve.com

France: 71 bis rue du Cardinal Lemoine, 75005 Paris
tel: 1 44 32 06 20 fax: 1 46 34 72 55
e-mail: 100560.415@compuserve.com

World Wide Web: Lonely Planet is now accesible via the World
Wide Web. For travel information and an up-to-date catalogue, you
can find us at http://www.lonelyplanet.com/

THE LONELY PLANET STORY

Lonely Planet published its first book in 1973 in response to the numerous 'How did you do it?' questions Maureen and Tony Wheeler were asked after driving, bussing, hitching, sailing and railing their way from England to Australia.

Written at a kitchen table and hand collated, trimmed and stapled, *Across Asia on the Cheap* became an instant local bestseller, inspiring thoughts of another book.

Eighteen months in South-East Asia resulted in their second guide, *South-East Asia on a shoestring*, which they put together in a backstreet Chinese hotel in Singapore in 1975. The 'yellow bible' as it quickly became known to backpackers around the world, soon became *the* guide to the region. It has sold well over half a million copies and is now in its 8th edition, still retaining its familiar yellow cover.

Today there are over 180 titles, including travel guides, walking guides, language kits & phrasebooks, travel atlases and travel literature. The company is one of the largest travel publishers in the world. Although Lonely Planet initially specialised in guides to Asia, we now cover most regions of the world, including the Pacific, North America, South America, Africa, the Middle East and Europe.

The emphasis continues to be on travel for independent travellers. Tony and Maureen still travel for several months of each year and play an active part in the writing, updating and quality control of Lonely Planet's guides.

They have been joined by over 70 authors and 170 staff at our offices in Melbourne (Australia), Oakland (USA), London (UK) and Paris (France). Travellers themselves also make a valuable contribution to the guides through the feedback we receive in thousands of letters each year.

The people at Lonely Planet strongly believe that travellers can make a positive contribution to the countries they visit, both through their appreciation of the countries' culture, wildlife and natural features, and through the money they spend. In addition, the company makes a direct contribution to the countries and regions it covers. Since 1986 a percentage of the income from each book has been donated to ventures such as famine relief in Africa; aid projects in India; agricultural projects in Central America; Greenpeace's efforts to halt French nuclear testing in the Pacific; and Amnesty International.

'I hope we send the people out with the right attitude about travel. You realise when you travel that there are so many different perspectives about the world, so we hope these books will make people more interested in what they see.'

— Tony Wheeler